ITALY FEVER

ITALY FEVER

*14 Ways to Satisfy
Your Love Affair with Italy*

DARLENE MARWITZ

Portico Press, Inc.
Fredericksburg, Texas

For information, contact Portico Press, Inc.,
P. O. Box 1337
Fredericksburg, TX 78624

Please visit our Web site.
www.italyfever.com

The author gratefully acknowledges *The Art of Pilgrimage: The
Seeker's Guide to Making Travel Sacred* by Phil Cousineau.
Copyright © 1998 by Conari Press. Excerpt reprinted by permis-
sion of Conari Press via Copyright Clearance Center.

Library of Congress Catalog Card Number 99-61406
ISBN 0-9664998-2-4

Jacket design by ROB JOHNSON
Book design by STEPHEN BRIGHT
Additional photography by the author
Printed in the United States of America

FIRST PRINTING
OCTOBER 1999

10 9 8 7 6 5 4 3 2 1

To my husband, David,
for intuitively being there for me
at every moment when I most wanted
to toss it all away

And to my mother, Letha Sheldon,
for instilling in me
the gift of stick-to-it-ness

CONTENTS

Preface

Courting a love affair with a European country is impractical for me, to say the least. Insane, irrational. I've heard it all. My husband attributes my Italian fling to what he calls "artistic temperament." He shakes his head and peers at me over his glasses in silence, tolerating the presence of a foreign intruder in our home.

My obsession with Italy began in August of 1988 while traveling with a fellow graduate student in pursuit of quintessential Italian architecture. It was a sojourn like thousands of others made by American students in their mystical trips abroad to study ancient Roman ruins and grand palatial masterpieces of the Italian Renaissance.

With forethought and struggle, my friend Linda and I plotted our travels—each step landing with purpose. Italy was our dream tour, a fitting finale to a summer of study abroad, our chance to be baptized in the architectural birthplace of our historic preservation studies. We dreamed of *palazzi* with softly colored frescoes, tile-roofed stone villas amid cypress-topped hills, and fragments of Roman antiquity dancing between light and shadow—the picturesque landscape and architecture of our beloved Italy.

Obsessing on Italy is relentless. Each day I uncover new writers, old writers, great writers who share my passion. Each week I meet others who have traveled to, lived in, or desire to go to Italy. Each fellow Italy lover fuels me forward into something bigger than was first imagined. Possessed by the romance and mystery of a country that holds few secrets from the centuries of travelers and writers before me, I often questioned my reasons for pursuing this project. Why write about a destination so far from home? Why *dare* to write about a place that writers of note have been describing for hundreds of years?

But my response, always, is more declaration than answer. If it's easy, why do it at all? If longings are weak, where is the challenge? I write about loving Italy because it is what I *choose* to do at this time in my life. For me.

When passion exists, I believe it is possible to follow grand goals wherever they lead. I'm fortunate. My mother taught me to dream big at an early age, then demonstrated, over the course of many years, her own commitment to goal setting—eventually teaching her *first* class of first-grade students at the age of sixty-five. Writing about Italy seemed mild in comparison to facing a room full of children at 8 o'clock every morning.

If my passion for Italy is out of control, I'm not alone. *The New York Times* reported that the number of Americans journeying to the hills of Tuscany doubled in three years, reaching 600,000 a few years ago. Catapulted by the 1996 release of *Under the Tuscan Sun*, Frances Mayes' mega-terrific bestseller, Tuscany continues to be the dream destination for thousands of Americans. And to think that this region is but a single piece of the delightful puzzle. As a sunny magnet drawing spellbound visitors, Italy lures us with its magical combination of chaos and charm. Larger than the state of Arizona but smaller than Japan, Italy exceeds expectations. Few destinations rival the romantic lure of Italian coastlines and lakes, Tuscan hillsides, Venetian waterways, and the remains of a Roman empire.

Realizing that my desire to partake of Italy is far from unique, I offer this collection of explorations as a reflection and response to my own experiences, my own desires—in hopes of expanding the realm of journey for others. The message herein is intended as a means of helping readers, whether traveling vicariously or planning a trip in earnest, to discover the yearnings, fuel the flame, fulfill their own dreams of Italy.

In no way am I able to capture even a fraction of what is grand and intimate about Italy. I make no attempt to do so except in terms of my personal aspirations and private love affair with this country. I've never lived in Italy, nor do I have longtime acquaintances who live there. Instead, my expertise lies in my passion, the knowledge I seek about all things Italian—stemming from my first glimpse of a Renaissance villa in Vicenza, Palladio's Villa Rotonda. It was love at first sight, not only for what the villa displayed architecturally, but for what it represented in spirit to me.

Feeding my fever for Italy forced me to see the renaissance that was taking place in my own life—a post-forty reawakening, a rebirth, a quest for revitalized consciousness and appreciation of simple pleasures. As a pre-travel companion, this book offers simple inspiration for pursuing passion: old and new ideas and humble experiences to help readers discover, interpret, and incorporate the intrinsic pleasures of Italy, while nurturing spirits for forthcoming journeys—whether in mind or body.

Update Passports and Luggage

I love to travel. My husband does not. I pack too little and he packs too much. While David despises all manner of overnight accommodation, I'm happy to pull together a little black bag at a moment's notice.

Unlike me, my spouse will do almost anything to avoid confrontation with a suitcase, conjuring any action or scheme that allows him to sidestep the issue altogether. With spousal finesse and political creativity, he delivers eloquent excuses like a politician dodging a tax bill. He knows how to flip-flop my proposals for adventure so that he comes out on top.

"I really think you'll get more out of this research trip if you go to New York by yourself," he said, almost two years ago.

I'd asked my husband to join me for an Italian excursion—opera, dining, shopping. As usual, he was right about a solo trip being better for me, but I accused him of not wanting to pack. (How dare he be a saint on my behalf when he's doing what *he* wants to do!)

To me, it's a sad state of travel affairs that my husband has no relationship with a piece of luggage. None. And he's the only person I know who possessed a passport for nine years before getting it stamped the first time. The only reason it even existed was that I insisted he get one, in case something happened to me while I was in Europe.

In contrast, since their European initiation many years ago, my backpack and passport beg to be used: "Take me. Take us. Get a ticket and we'll go." They constantly plead to be jostled, abused, inspected, and stamped or tagged with cryptic destinations.

A few years ago, when I realized that both our passports were soon due to expire, Italy beckoned with resounding lure. Obviously, I needed no luring myself. But David? Getting him to the airport with a passport in hand would be major-league action, a game worthy of record attendance. Like the farmer in the movie who builds a baseball diamond in the middle of a cornfield, hoping fans will come, I kept thinking, "If I build and present a good story, will David go with me to Italy?"

With high hopes and purpose, creating, building, pushing to the edge, I outlined and embellished multiple scenarios—compelling reasons for us to go to Italy *now*. Then, I bribed. "If you go this year for our twentieth anniversary, I'll get you that canine buddy you've always wanted." For nearly twenty years my husband has told anyone who will listen about how he'd love to have a dog, but that I'm against the idea. He runs the whole string of words together to make it sound like the title of a country western song: "I Really Want a Dog but My Wife Won't Let Me Have One."

Reinforcing my offer of a dog (and to prevent the possibility of a family addition that would rival a horse—my husband's idea of a *real* dog), I scouted for svelte Italian dog breeds on the Internet. If it took a barking pet to get my spouse to go to Italy, then why not an Italian puppy?

Finally, creative stories exhausted (and puppy postponed), it worked. After twenty years of marriage and against my better judgment, I finally convinced David to use his virgin passport and our frequent flyer miles to celebrate a special anniversary in the country of cypress-fringed roads and blood-orange sunsets.

As soon as he agreed, however, my heart began fluttering with anticipation—but not for the reason you might expect. It wasn't that I was already daydreaming of a tangled Tuscan romance in a country villa. Instead, I was struck by the thought of David trying to pack clothes for his first trip abroad. Getting him to go was one thing, but packing? Suddenly, I panicked. I'd never be able to convince him to pack just one bag. Or would I?

Whether planning a dream trip to Italy or not, the simple act of packing will either convince you to continue with your vision, or else prompt you to abort foreign travel for a backyard destination. As soon as a suitcase gets dug out of the back of our closet, a hidden vacation meter starts ticking in the house. Each zip of a pocket is a zip of anxiety—too many pouches to open and close, too many ridiculous places to swallow a sock, your favorite underwear, and the only belt with enough pre-punched holes to accommodate vacation food feasts.

"What's wrong with our old blue Samsonite with the lid you sit on to close?" asks David. "Is there a new luggage law I don't know about that requires a certain number of zippers per mile of intended travel? Some kind of frequent-zipper law?"

What was I thinking when I proposed this trip! Was I delusional at the time? Reminded of honeymoon bliss? Had my own desire to wander caused me to momentarily forget all previous vacation departures with David—"his" suitcases of every size, shape, and bowling-ball-bag impersonation? All the late-night hours of packing and repacking? How did I expect my husband to pack for a foreign country when he stuffs an overnight bag as if he were headed to the moon— worthy of worry like it was the last trip he'd ever take!

You may assume David is fussy about fashion. But he's not. The problem is his ardent enthusiasm—for cleanliness.

He showers twice a day. As a result, he packs two a day of everything he considers to be basic. Like a vendor on the streets of Manhattan, he lays out his goods on the bed for visual inspection: two shirts, two pants, two tee-shirts, two pairs each of underwear and socks, two belts, two handkerchiefs; you get the idea. Then, with a few "what if" situations tossed in, he further reduces all risk for spontaneous pleasure by adding more items to the mix for safe measure. No matter how you look at it, he's a lousy packer, a miserable traveler. He's destined for some famous list.

"But what will I do if it's cooler than expected?" he asks. "Should I take a few long sleeve shirts, or only short sleeve shirts and a jacket?"

Taking a deep breath and faking a smile, I respond. "Why not carry a light jacket to layer with your shirts—no matter the length of your sleeves? I believe coats were designed for unexpected cool weather." Unfortunately, he catches the sarcasm that slips through my lips.

"*Thank you* for being so kind and understanding," he replies. "I really appreciate your sincere effort in helping me pack."

I know better than to respond with an attitude, but I can't help it. The long versus short sleeve dilemma is a twenty-year routine with us. It's like playing "shirt scrabble" from a suitcase instead of a box—and always coming up with the same old words. Short sleeves, long sleeves. Long sleeves, short sleeves.

If I suggest, "Why don't you take all short sleeve shirts?", he says, "I think I'll take long sleeves." When I suggest, "Why don't you take long sleeve shirts?", he reaches for short sleeve ones instead. I'm convinced he doesn't really want my opinion, yet he's annoyed if I don't play the game.

In addition to basics, my husband packs specialized gear and clothing for every conceivable activity or situation that can possibly be identified at the stroke of midnight—his packing hour of choice. His favorite leisure sport, cycling, requires thousands of bicycle-specific treasures for the suitcase: padded spandex shorts, sweat-wicking jerseys with back pockets, fingertipless gloves, a safety helmet with vents, shoes with lock-in clips, water bottles that squirt, energy snacks, spare tubes, a tire pump, an odometer, assorted tools, and a dozen sweat bands—one to be worn while packing!

It's specialized gear and clothing that unfortunately doesn't lend itself well in a pinch. Usually that's me—in a pinch. I mean. I'm the one always borrowing clothes from David. And it's seldom hassle-free.

"What's wrong?" he says. "Clothes all dirty? Didn't pack enough to wear?"

"No, not at all. That's not it," I lie, while secretly scanning my husband's open bag for possibilities. If I borrow his bicycle shoes with metal fittings in the soles, I'll sound like an old gray mare—clip-clop, clip-clop, across the *piazza*. If I negotiate for one of David's bicycle shirts—mostly advertisement-ridden with shocking bicycle-team colors—I'll look like a walking billboard. And if I plead for a spare pair of his padded bicycle shorts, because I didn't pack sports clothes at all, then I'll look like Humpty Dumpty—too rounded in all the wrong places.

What good does it do for him to pack all these clothes? I can't wear a single thing!

David's travel philosophy is simple: pack it all, and *big* and *more* is better. It's inherent thinking for the men in his family—passed from father to son, generation to generation.

For every joint trip undertaken, David's response to my astonishment is the same. "What difference does it make how many bags I take as long as I carry them myself?" But I can see where it's headed. A taxi will be useless. We'll soon need a moving van to cart us home intact from the airport.

My logic is different. My rule is to carry one piece of luggage, no matter the distance. A hundred miles for one night, or thousands of miles for weeks—one bag. Dallas, New York, or Italy—one bag. What doesn't fit in my little black pack stays at home.

Again, where was the sanity check when I proposed this trip? What was I *thinking*?

For months before introducing the idea of Italy, I tried to figure out how to make separate vacations sound attractive for our forthcoming anniversary. I rationalized that all twenty-year couples are entitled to, and by outward appearances deserving of, independent relaxation. Shouldn't two decades be the endurance limit in a marriage for communal vacations?

Then I changed my mind. I worried how it would sound and look to our friends and family. I could hear the comments already.

"You're going to do *what* on your anniversary?" David's parents would query with puzzled faces. "You're not going together?"

"You're taking *separate* vacations?" my mother would ask. "Is there something else you're not telling me?"

If it sounds crazy that I contemplated an anniversary trip alone, then you've never accompanied my husband, never spotted him at an airport. One sighting of him with his baggage entourage is all it would take for you to appreciate my position.

The fact that David associates travel with work (he frequently has to travel on business) makes matters worse. As a result, he'd rather stay at home, or at least close to home. He's the only person I know who didn't get excited about the prospect of going to Italy—at least not at first. Even with free tickets, I had to convince him.

"Why don't we go to West Texas? Fort Davis and Big Bend National Park. Can't we just *drive* somewhere for our twentieth anniversary?" His initial response made it obvious that my work was cut out for me with this Italy trip. It called for a genuine *plan*. If I talked it up too much too soon, David was sure to balk. The worrying would start and he'd get skittish about the packing—nine months ahead of schedule, nine months too soon.

In the midst of my own worrying, it finally hit me: Italy is *my* passion, not his. David's leisure-time fervor was cycling!

When I finally realized I was going about this trip idea all wrong, my mind started scheming, pumping new thoughts—insidious, but well-meaning, thoughts. Sentences thereafter were plotted and planted with bicycle-trip-sounding words.

"You know that Italian bicycle you ride?" I said, probing with care. "I'll bet we could visit the Tommasini factory. I think it's at Grosseto, near Siena—in Tuscany. That might be kind of fun, don't you think? We could see where your bicycle was made!" David's ears perked at the mention of his Tommasini. So I tossed out another worm. "Isn't there a velodrome in Milan? I thought I heard you mention it a few months ago."

Yes, yes. I knew I'd cast fat bait when his response fell into place as predicted. "Did you say we might go to Milan?" he asked. "Hmm. Maybe we could find the Campagnola factory, too. I've been wanting some "Campi" parts. I wonder what city they're in?"

"I don't know, but I'm sure it'll be easy to find out!"

Cunning and artful thinking was working. David was now pondering the possibility of scattered bicycle excursions, instead of dreading an anniversary trip too far from home. He even sounded a little excited.

But now I worried. Had I outsmarted myself? From past experience, I knew about the associated bulk of close-to-home bicycling with David—plenty of baggage in tow for cycling gear when we transported our bikes to ride in nearby towns. But a foreign bicycle trip? The image of David armored with Samsonite like a caddy carrying golf clubs was not my dream of Italy. The ominous quickly turned obvious. I must next convince David to travel *light*—with only one bag, one small enough to be carried on board. Checked luggage was to be avoided at all cost!

The sheer thought of baggage separation made me queasy. As hard as it would be for David to shrink his belongings into one carry-on, I knew losing his possessions would be even more stressful, more frustrating for him (and for me!). Could I deal with a husband with lost luggage—in a foreign country?

I also knew that depending on public laundries in Italy was impossible. So when David said, "Guess I'll just have to be satisfied taking things to a Laundromat when they get dirty," I changed the subject. I wasn't about to tell him that I'd never seen a commercial laundry in Italy—not one. There had been plenty in England and France, but I didn't have a clue where Italians washed their clothes.

Primary strategy: I started saving David's old underwear, the ragged ones with holes and stretched-out elastic.

16

Instead of "wash and wear," my plan was to "wear and toss." But I also knew it was imperative to lighten David's load *before* leaving. Tossing along the way would never be enough, and always be a challenge. I could hear the words now, drifting through an open window onto a back street in Siena, "Oh, no. I can't possibly throw *that* pair of underwear away. There's only a tiny hole in the seat. What if I need another spare pair?"

"Okay, okay. Keep five spares for two more days. It's your decision," I lie, before discreetly discarding a few old Jockeys in a wadded paper sack at the bottom of a trash can.

Don't get me wrong. I have nothing against wearing clean underwear. It's actually my preference. But without hesitation I'm more than willing to get a little dirty if that's what it takes to travel with ease.

Tossing all manner of fashion in reckless abandon—carrying one bag on our backs and a small pack on our shoulders—our twentieth anniversary trip to the Veneto and Tuscany regions was planned with bicycling activities to entice a reluctant-to-travel husband, and as a repeat architectural tour for me.

Dreaming about Italy is easier when you fondle and cradle the little blue book that makes foreign excursion possible—

the exotic though often elusive passport. Is yours stuck or hidden in a drawer? If so, dig it out. Check its expiration. Irresistible travel deals often arrive without notice, and frequent flyer miles add up sooner than you'd think.

And luggage? Use your crush on Italy as an excuse to go shopping. A new piece of luggage to accompany your passport places travel in perspective. Investigate keen baggage styles with dozens of pockets and wheels like skates. Inspect one of those serious backpacks with a hip belt for distributing weight. If in doubt, get it all! Buy one of the new multipurpose bags—one with straps, handles, pockets, wheels, and a hip belt.

In preparation for our special Italy trip, David and I experimented with various sizes, configurations, and weight conditions before settling on gear that suited us. Like giant sea turtles waddling toward water, we loaded them up with books, clothes, and junk from around the house before starting out for the evening—making the rounds in the neighborhood, getting used to our soft-shelled profiles.

Every few blocks, we'd stop to pull and tuck each other's straps, shift weight, and circle back home to eliminate something before heading out again with lighter loads and new conviction. Quickly, we learned that precious amenities lose value and that indispensable items become dispensable—when traveling like a tortoise with a house on your back.

Display Maps As Art

I Darlene Sheldon Marwitz, shall be solely responsible for all future vacations, good and bad, throughout our married life. I don't remember saying those words during our wedding vows over twenty years ago, but David swears I did. Was I delirious, in love, not thinking ahead—not thinking at all? In retrospect, I should have demanded an answer to "Will you love, honor, and please travel with me?" Only now is it clear to me that individuals should have the right to know, ahead of time and in writing, whether or not their partner for life likes to travel. And the answer should be written in blood.

After two decades of marriage as chief planner, navigator, and the "one who likes to go places" in the family, one thing is ongoing and clear. When something goes wrong on vacation, it's always my fault. When a thunderstorm appears without warning while touring Georgia O'Keeffe's house in Abiquiu, New Mexico, it's my fault for lugging one umbrella, not two. When a gentle summer breeze suddenly turns cold in Jackson Hole, Wyoming, it's my fault for toting a cap and a hat, not nylon windbreakers with hoods.

Uniform long gone but a Girl Scout for life, I'm perpetually prepared for emergencies. And my ever-present handbag yields a ton of stuff to prove it. Every item I carry either digs, slices, screws, anoints, nourishes, navigates, or otherwise performs active duty.

Being prepared, however, has its price. Over the years David has come to expect that my strapped-on purse is bottomless, weightless, and carried on his behalf. Like magic, every conceivable object for *his* convenience is supposed to appear from my shouldered bag of tricks. Every woman who's ever been asked to slip something small into her handbag recognizes the frustration of hearing: "Would you mind keeping my sunglasses in your purse?"

After dog-earing dozens of catalog pages months before our anniversary trip to Italy, I finally figured out how to remedy the magic bag situation. I ordered new travel duds for David. Two shirts and two pairs of pants: super-duper, miracle-fiber shirts boasting dozens of pockets, and ingenious, gear-toting, cargo pants with snaps, buttons, zippers, and pockets up and down each leg.

By default, I still carry the maps in our family, but my husband now manages his own sundry items and is happy to do so.

Maybe it's because our sense of geography is so poor that David and I like the idea of maps tacked on our walls, used for reference while reading. Years ago, longing for a set of old-fashioned "school maps" (the ones that mount on a wall and pull down like roller shades), we searched map and antique shops but were unable to locate the spring-loaded variety. Since then, we've settled for simple laminated selections and inexpensive folding ones—the latter being the kind of map that refuses to refold in reverse order of how it was opened!

But the Italy maps on our walls belong to me. Far from being hidden in an out-of-the-way place, one primary map holds a prominent position at the top of our stairs—impossible to ignore. We walk by it a dozen times a day. I study. Peruse. Drool. Talk to it. David passes by it in silence, ignoring the outline of a boot that has become art on our walls.

Other cartographic displays also line our stairwell like a travel trunk boasting stickers from around the world. In the way that artwork prompts conversation, our mapped-out staircase provides entertainment with friends. Like being stuck on an elevator with nothing to do but push buttons, we hover in cramped quarters on the steps and landings, trying to decipher writing too small to read, attempting to recall basic geography: "Would you look at this? I never realized Ireland was *north* of Maine. And where did this little flyspeck of a country come from? Is it one of those countries with a new name, or am I totally forgetful?"

Either the little things in life don't count at all or they count for everything. For me, the subtleties of Italy are paramount, and my push-pinned map helps me decide where to dig for the details I crave. I claim new spots by circling them in ink, each looped inch a gold mine for exploration. If I read about a spa, such as Grotta Giusti at Monsummano Terme, I'll circle its location on the map near Pistóia, northeast of Florence. If I read about a grand patrician garden, perhaps the one hidden behind estate walls at Villa Allegri Arvedi in the Veneto, I'll circumscribe its position north of Verona. If I catch but a glimpse of Isola Bella while watching *Victory Garden* on TV, then I'll research its whereabouts on Lake Maggiore and surround it with another ring. Often it's the complexity and concentration of inked goose eggs on my map that best helps me define a new itinerary.

In addition to circling, I write on maps. Scribbling notes next to cities and other sites puts me in control. Without personal markings, the graphed and charted documents remain foreign, untouchable. My advice is to lay claim to a new map as soon as you get one. Talk to your map. Repeat the strange names of new cities until they're familiar. Circle favorite locations you know a little about but wish to learn more. Use colored pencils to highlight special regions— "sienna brown" or "tuscan red" for Tuscany, "mediterranean blue" for the Veneto, "light umber" for Umbria. Take charge of your map; don't allow intimidation. Study it like the plan of your house so you can maneuver it in the dark without stumping your toe while dreaming.

For the moment, I display a general map of Italy where the cities are identified in Italian: Roma, Milano, and Venezia, not Rome, Milan, Venice. The local names are intriguing and mysterious, rolling off the tongue with obvious foreign flair. It used to bother me that not all major cities and towns in Italy had English versions of their names. "Where's the continuity!" I'd ask. But with time, I've accepted this mix of identifiers as yet another Italian idiosyncrasy, a likable one in truth. Shamelessly romantic, I find solace in visiting places where English names don't mark the landscape.

Once you're oriented with the overall layout and principal cities of Italy, good regional and local maps are essential for delving into lesser known territories—the smallest quaint towns and outlying *campagna*, or rural, sites. Visitors to southern regions can associate their travels with the toe or heel of Italy's boot, but central and northern locations (where I like to roam) are less easily referenced. Unlike the toe or heel, referring to the calf or shin of the

Italian boot sounds both odd and unromantic: "Having a great time in the shin of Italy—going farther up the calf tomorrow. Wish you were here!"

Placing travel in perspective in central and northern regions is more challenging than in the south. But my method is simple. Ignoring kilometers and reverting to miles, I calculate the distance between cities by the width and reach of my hands. A quick hand-over-hand motion across the contour of a map gives me a measure I comprehend. One closed width of my hand (fingers not flared) is about 160 miles on a map with a scale of one centimeter to ten kilometers (1 cm = 10 km). And with fully spread fingers my reach is more than 300 miles. The downside of thinking in terms of *miles*, however, is that mileage and travel time don't compare well between Texas and Italy. In Texas a hundred miles is a quick trip to visit friends, but not so in Italy. There, I'm always thinking I'll get somewhere faster than I really can.

Of course, the best place to find good maps is in Italy. Each time I travel I stock up on new ones, making room in my bag by ditching tired clothes. Worn-out pajamas, or gaudy ones received for Christmas from well-meaning relatives, especially make ideal traveling companions. Nobody sees you wear them and you don't feel guilty when you leave them behind!

Attention grabbers are the De Agostini series of regional maps and the Touring Club Italiano selections. I pick up city maps too—often the Piante di Città editions by Studio F. M. B. Bologna. So *what* if you can buy many of the same maps in the States! Buying them in Italy is more fun.

The real gems, however, are the local offerings. Major cities for sure, but even smaller *paesi*, or towns, often provide beautiful indigenous maps or specialized guides. A colorful illustrated map and pamphlet in English and Italian, "The Villas of Andrea Palladio in the Province of Vicenza," is but one of my architecture-specific, and now hoarded, discoveries. On site is where you fall in love with a map's markings, contours, and place names—in the shadow of a *palazzo* or villa, in the midst of an Italian *giardino*, within the heartbeat of a city *piazza*.

Reading about mapmaking is also rewarding. A class assignment in architecture school one year was to read Italo Calvino's *Invisible Cities*. Not only was the book my introduction to the Italian writer; it also exposed me to a wonderfully concocted meditation—Calvino's interpretation of Marco Polo's description of his expeditions (as told to Kublai Khan). For the project, each student was required to read Calvino's medley of city descriptions, and then create a map or interpretive layout of the one we liked best.

I chose "Esmeralda." Real or not, it reminded me of Venice. A city of canals with "tortuous optional routes," according to Calvino, a place where zigzagging to destinations was common. Therefore, my stylized map of Esmeralda assumed the guise of a woven rug, an Oriental carpet with knotted pathways connecting colorful arabesque motifs.

More recently, I've enjoyed another cartographic adventure by reading James Cowan's historical work of fiction, *A Mapmaker's Dream: The Meditations of Fra Mauro, Cartographer to the Court of Venice.* Though the book is shorter than its name, it's not a quick read. Each word must be swallowed, regurgitated, and swallowed again. The concept of how a mapmaker translates images in the mind to images on paper is staggering to contemplate.

My personal interest in tacking maps on a wall stems from maternal roots. I'm accustomed to my mother's habit of routinely keeping a map or some kind chart on display. A few years ago during the Gulf War, she posted a map of Middle Eastern countries on her dining room wall—an impossible location to ignore in her house— next to a tiny blue cap that hangs on a nail. The cap is a Cub Scout cap from the 1960s that belonged to my brother Dennis. And while guests never hesitate to ask about the cap, they never know whether to ask about the map or not. I assume they think it odd that a woman in a small rural town in Texas is interested in a Mid-East Crisis map primarily showing Iran, Iraq, Saudi Arabia, and Israel.

Mother's map, however, is not alarming to me. Nothing she reads or studies surprises me anymore; any subject is of potential interest. Hasn't everyone's mother read Thomas Friedman's *From Beirut to Jerusalem* in the last few years? Doesn't every mother keep a geological chart of fossils taped on her kitchen cabinet door—a refresher course in action every time one reaches for a glass?

I confess. My devotion to maps often gets me into trouble. Out of habit I collect multiple maps for major trips: various scales, assorted versions, some too tiny to decipher, a few too large to unfold in a car without posing danger. But each one tells me something different—details I want to know whether I need to know them or not.

Clairvoyance is hardly required to see the obvious problem with shuffling too many maps on the go. By the time I pinpoint the most useful information, the most useful crossroad is whizzing by in a blur. "Oh, there it is," I say. "*That* was the road we needed to take. Can you turn around and go back?"

But my role as chief navigator in the family should not be bumped for excessive map juggling. And if you ask why, the answer is simple: I don't mind turning a car around to find the road that's needed, and I'm perfectly capable of asking for directions. I'm content to try and try again until

I get it right, while my husband's solution is to *explore* a new route. At the wheel, David thinks he's Christopher Columbus. Never mind that his *discovery* is out of the way by a few counties or fifty miles—any solution is better to him than turning back or requesting assistance.

According to Erma Bombeck (whose wisdom increases as I grow older), "men never ask directions" and they never get lost. Since I happen to have married a clone of her husband as she described him in 1969, I salute her analysis and conclusion. But things could be worse. In truth, I know they'll get worse in a few more years. Not only does David's father never ask for directions, he doesn't believe in stopping anywhere that's on the left side of the road. If it's not on the right, then forget it. Convinced that my husband inherited from his father's right-side-of-the-road gene pool, I'm trying to do all the left-side-of-the-road stuff now.

The last time I had trouble with a map was in Venice—on the honeymoon vacation for which I was responsible. Following the advice of a guidebook that said "Just get lost," I did, with David in tow. We roamed, circled, and crisscrossed—up and down bridge after bridge. Plan or no plan, it's what one does in Venice, where the city's four hundred or so bridges define distance. Venetians live ninty-nine bridges from the train station, twenty-six bridges from the closest shoe repair shop, or six bridges from their favorite bar.

Like experimental test rats, we explored the myriad of mazes before us, turning around at dead ends, taking alternate paths as required. After locating the burned-down opera house, La Fenice, by the sight of a construction crane veering overhead—a looming giraffe sticking its neck above the crowd—there was nothing left to do that was tickling my mind. And that was the idea. Going to Venice without a plan was indeed the plan I'd made.

But as soon as David suggested we return to the train station, after only two hours in a Venice even more crowded with tourists than usual (all of us having arrived on Monday to avoid a weekend anti-secessionist demonstration), I thought about Harry's Bar. Where *was* Harry's Bar?

It wasn't that we intended to stop for a drink, or that otherwise it would have been a big item on our agenda if we had one. But on the spur of the moment, wouldn't it be fun to see this legendary literary spot, the bar made famous by Ernest Hemingway? We could talk about it later with bookloving friends from Manhattan who were coming to Venice on the heels of our trip. It was "touristy," yes, but no one we knew was watching. And how long could it possibly take to find it? A few minutes?

So there we were, in search of Harry's Bar—without a map, or at least not much of one. Randomly, I stumbled across snippets of information, "pieces" of maps on different pages in a guidebook. On one page Harry's Bar was listed with a bold alphabet letter beside it as a "key," but no indication of how the key was connected to a map. And which map? The map section on the adjoining page was noted with numbers, not letters. Where was the ABC and XYZ map? Was I thumbing through some kind of "Sherlock" guidebook in which you're given one clue at a time?

"Okay," I said, giving up on random page-flipping. "I'll go straight to the index." But instead of yielding the ideal map, the designated page told me how to make peach bellinis—one-fourth measure of peach juice to three-fourths measure of Prosecco wine. However nice it was to know how to make bellinis for the next time I had a "Harry's Bar Party," the recipe was not very useful in getting us to the spot where the famous drinks were served.

David was nearing his threshold of patience. He didn't appreciate my dilemma with the guidebook, yet he wasn't offering to give it a go himself. He was tired of the tourists, tired of me. So I didn't make a big deal of it when he surrendered with the suggestion that we—rather I—ask for help. "Why don't you ask inside the store where we bought the last postcards? How hard can it be to find Harry's Bar? Surely they can tell us how to get there from here."

"Follow to the end of this street," the saleswoman explained as she pointed in a general direction, "and turn left. Then proceed straight ahead past the basilica and the Palazzo Ducale and this will take you to Harry's." It sounded simple, though I wasn't sure what qualified as a "street" in a city without cars.

Walking and turning as directed, we soon ended up at the water's edge. The Grand Canal lay before us, souvenir vendors scattered themselves to our left, and something called the Royal Gardens was farther down on the right. But a bar? We backtracked to see where we'd gone wrong, searching for a sign that would mark the spot, expecting something bold—boldly American. Maybe neon?

Next, my jaw dropped as I watched David (the one who never asks for help) hail two pistol-packing *carabinieri* like he was hailing a cab. First I cringed. Then I tried not to laugh.

The scene was a comical act between dissimilar characters. The officers expressed confusion and compassion with pronounced facial expressions, but couldn't interpret David's question with its Texas twist. Frustrated, they flagged a third officer to join the sidewalk conference, but again to no avail. Amid hand motions and a flurry of foreign words—both Texan and Italian—the policemen finally shook their heads for the last time, smiled politely, and walked away. We were left again, back where we started, in search of Harry's Bar.

Finding the bar was now a quest. Something that was relatively unimportant to us when we started the adventure suddenly assumed the guise of a fierce opponent—one to be conquered.

After cruising the Piazzetta San Marco like players in a board game that doesn't end, after crossing the Ponte della Paglia (the Bridge of Straw) on more occasions than I care to admit while sighing my own sighs at the Ponte dei Sospiri (the famous Bridge of Sighs), and after circling like buzzards with the ubiquitous pigeons on the Piazza San Marco, I finally uncovered a second, albeit skinny, guidebook hidden in the bottom of my backpack. After all else failed, I read simple directions about like this: "When you get out at the San Marco stop, Harry's Bar is straight ahead." This time, something that sounded easy *was* easy. We traced our steps all the way back to the *vaporetto* stop, looked right and left, and then behind us to spot Hemingway's famous "American" bar smack-dab in our face.

"But where's the sign?" David said. "Can you believe there's no sign? Only a little gold lettering on the glass spelling out Harry's Bar."

"And it's vertical! Who reads anything up and down anymore? No wonder we missed it when we landed this morning."

Complaining about the lack of signage made me feel better and offered a sense of closure. But instead of entering the bar we'd seemingly spent hours searching for, we stepped up to validate our tickets and boarded the #82 *vaporetto* headed for the station where we would catch the next train to Vicenza. Seeing the outside of the bar had been enough. Mission completed, we said good-bye to Venice—me, clicking away with my camera as we slowly motored along the Grand Canal, and David, content to sit and absorb the *palazzi* panorama before us. As if we were watching an epic silent movie in reverse order, the *vaporetto* returned us to the opening scene.

Travel Through Movies

avid and I still go to "picture shows," not movies, and when we go it's a special occasion. Having grown up together in a community where you had to drive to nearby small towns for an indoor or drive-in theater, we thought of going to the picture show as an *event*—not the sanitized version of movie watching that goes on today, sitting in cookie-cutter cineplexes, strangers in the dark.

More than anything else except books, picture shows exposed us to the outside world. In 1969, David and I were fledgling sweethearts caught up in the tie-dyed and leather-fringed image and music of Woodstock—Santana, Janis Joplin, Joan Baez, Joe Cocker, Creedence Clearwater

Revival, Blood, Sweat and Tears. At the same time, we were living with pickups and rodeos and Friday night football. But our real travel experiences arrived that year in the guise of two movies. *Easy Rider* and *Midnight Cowboy*.

We were too young to drive and too young to be admitted, but somehow David maneuvered his mother into taking us to see *Easy Rider* at a drive-in theater twenty-five miles away. In spite of our age, there was no question about getting in; we had a parent in tow. And the next thing that happened was too convenient to believe. Quickly bored with the movie, David's mother switched places with us to move to the back seat where, rather instantly, she fell asleep.

To the beat of "Born to Be Wild," David and I followed the odyssey and drug-induced hallucinations of two long-haired, hippie bikers on a cross-country trip that shocked Hollywood and the nation. It would have shocked David's mother too had she been awake to see it!

Along about the same time, in another small town where we didn't typically go to the show, we saw *Midnight Cowboy* with an X-rating that made the R-rated *Easy Rider* pale. This time David managed to dupe a sister-in-law into taking us, after probably having told our parents it was a western! I was fourteen, David was thirteen, and our first impression of New York City was a sordid exploration of bartered sex and male prostitutes. As a shocking slice of pop culture for its time, *Midnight*

Cowboy reinforced our perception that picture shows were truly something to remember.

Today, my feverish interpretation of "Italian" movies is personal, eclectic, biased by small-town upbringing. It denotes foreign and domestic films that depict Italy in both big and small ways—not strictly Italian productions. The selections vary in genre, tone, rating, and film location, but the list is by no means definitive. (See Movies That Depict Italy.)

Demanding primary attention are several of the exotic neorealistic films, popularized by famous Italian directors like De Sica and Fellini, with characteristic actors such as Marcello Mastroianni and Sophia Loren. They dominate and seduce with a style of their own. In that they represent the classic Italian movie, Italian cinema would be lacking without them. Yet I also like movies that show me, tell me, something intimate or grand about Italy—the beauty or condition of the country and its people. Simple stories.

Noted with geographical context, the titles I've collected are a mix of movies generally available on video, some more difficult to locate than others. Entire movies were filmed on location in many cases. Minimal Italian scenery exists in others. Either way, the inclusion of a movie is personal preference. For one reason or another, I find a particular motion picture to be enlightening for armchair travel. Whether chosen for cinematographic achievement, for dispelling simple Italian charm, or for yet another quirky or romantic reason, the selections are ones I happen to like—no matter the caliber of industry recognition or the degree to which Italy is depicted.

Even to my own amazement, a number of aberrations exist on the list—odd movies with only subtle connections to Italy. Included are motion pictures, such as *Big Night* and *Moonstruck*, which are void of authentic foreign settings but evoke essential elements of Italy: food, family, music or opera. Each movie, to me, has a simple, delightful message.

For film connoisseurs, Web sites today make it easy to search for Italian movies and festivals. The Venice Film Festival, based on the Lido (a strip of land a short watercraft ride from Venice), is the obvious festival destination for Italy lovers intrigued by the glamour of the motion picture industry. The vast cultural arts competition known as the Venice Biennale has maintained a longtime following with the international arts community since its beginning in the late-nineteenth century. And, the film portion of the event, typically called the Venice Film Festival but officially named *Mostra Internazionale d'Arte Cinematografica*, was added in 1932—the first of its kind in the world.

More than a year ago, finally making it to the Lido for the first time, I walked the boulevard along the beach to see its two grand hotels, the Hotel des Bains and Hotel Excelsior. As one of only three tourists within sight at the time, I couldn't begin to imagine how the place could ever come alive, when the only hint of activity was a truck dumping sand. Fresh sand for the onslaught of summer bathers sure to come. But as empty as the stretch of beach was, one worthy view was the ghost town of bathhouses facing the sea. Row after row, as far as I could see. Section after section of blue, green, and white bathhouses looking like little soldier huts at attention.

The Lido, I concluded (unless you're a brave, wealthy, and devoted film buff), is one stint of Italian travel best observed from the comfort of a recliner at home. To witness the legendary Lido, with its beach and bathhouse setting across from the Hotel des Bains, rent Visconti's film version of Thomas Mann's *Death in Venice*. Or, catch additional hotel views by watching Count Almasy (Ralph Fiennes) and Katherine (Kristin Scott Thomas) ignite their love affair in *The English Patient*. The Hotel des Bains substitutes for a Cairo hotel setting.

Then, when you're ready to satisfy longings for a real Italian film festival, head for the one in California's Marin County. It's been a perennial fall favorite in the Bay Area for more than twenty years, offering new debuts and classics with subtitles in English. The movies are typically shown on consecutive Saturdays.

Last year, one of my whirlwind tours of Italy cost me less than a hundred dollars, including food and drink, and I didn't use a single frequent-flyer mile to do it. Instead of flying, I drove. Local video stores served as travel agencies for the journey; instead of the Hotel des Bains, my 1930s habitat doubled as *albergo* and home base for two weeks of travel—at night and on weekends.

As if descending into Milan's Malpensa airport, I plunged in my car down a steep *collina* at Twelfth and Lamar Boulevard to land at a neighborhood video *bottega*. Then onward in traffic, like Rome departing for her August vacation, I traveled via Lamar for more stops at video stores.

Carrying ragged, torn pages from *VideoHound's Golden Movie Retriever*, I booked movie destinations matching the first leg of my circled and highlighted itinerary. But when I pulled out my passport for "stamping," the salesperson was unimpressed. Her enthusiasm for my travel plans was less than I'd expected. Still, I whispered, "*Grazie, arrivederci,*" as I paid and walked out the door.

Back to my "hotel" in the snug comfort of an over-stuffed leather *sedia*—a sprawling chair soon filled with pizza and biscotti crumbs and sticky *limonata* spills—and I'm ready for departure. One fabulous film festival, five romantic favorites.

The first stop is Venice to see Katherine Hepburn in *Summertime*. Miss Hepburn's naïve portrayal of Jane

Hudson, a 1950s spinster alone on vacation, is charming and innocent. I, too, am innocent watching Miss Hudson partake of Venetian delights while succumbing to the charms of a local shopkeeper (Rossano Brazzi). I smile when she smiles. I breathe deeply as she takes breath from the city of canals. I am lured by every step Miss Hudson takes; each is my own. When she inches backward, absent-mindedly falling into a canal while focusing her movie camera, I fall with her.

Hopelessly romantic, inflicted with what writer Kate Simon calls the "*Summertime* syndrome" in a short essay titled "For Women," I long for the mysterious pathways of Venice every time I return to this classic movie. Originally published in Kate Simon's *Italy: The Places in Between* (1970), "For Women" is more readily accessible in Alice Leccesse Powers' anthology, *Italy in Mind* (1997).

My second stop is Rome for more romance with Rossano Brazzi, and to toss a coin into the Fountain of Trevi with the assistance of Audrey Hepburn. Worth more than a coin and a dream, *Three Coins in the Fountain* is essential viewing for any romantic film festival that celebrates the Latium region. The seemingly more popular *Roman Holiday*, an Audrey Hepburn and Gregory Peck classic, is less appealing to me. Given the choice, between Rossano Brazzi or Gregory Peck, I'll choose Brazzi every time.

Next, I drift farther south in Italy to visit my *Gone with the Wind* hero, Clark Gable, in *It Started in Naples*, also starring Sophia Loren. The same young actor (Salvatore Cascio) that tagged along trying to sell cigarettes and other goods to Miss Hudson in *Summertime* is equally fetching as the young son of a nightclub stripper (Sophia Loren) in Naples.

I zoom back up the coastline, almost to Genoa, and my fourth destination is enchanted indeed. It's Portofino. The escapism of *Enchanted April* is undeniable. Basking vicariously in the sun as a gentle breeze ruffles my hair, I slow to the wine-sipping pace of Italy and visualize myself taking respite at this movie's hillside villa overlooking the Riviera di Levante—the Italian Riviera.

My final heart-tugging movie in this festival of romantic escapade is *Il Postino*. Between the intoxication of the music and poetry and the remoteness of a fishing village on an island called Isola Salina, north of Sicily, it's impossible to neglect this bittersweet tale of longing and desire. Doubly bitter is the knowledge that actor Massimo Troisi (Mario) died soon after the final shooting of this epic love story.

It's easy to get the hang of coordinating film festivals at home—how to best spend your video bucks on travel. While eclectic movie selections are simple to pull together, focused combinations are better. Try organizing by general genre—adventure, western, drama, foreign language, etc.

Better still, create "picture show events" with thematic content—romance, opera, crime, period settings, individual directors (Bertolucci, De Sica, Fellini, Rossellini, Visconti, Zeffirelli) or actors (Marcello Mastroianni, Sophia Loren, Anna Magnani). You decide. Spit out tickets on your computer as invitations to friends:

You Are Invited for a Free Weekend of Crime
"MAFIA MOVIE MADNESS"
The Godfather Trilogy and *Flight of the Innocent*
WHEN:
WHERE:
TIME:
Pizza provided but bring your own Italian beer or wine!

Or, following the critical success of *Life Is Beautiful* (winner of three Academy Awards for 1998), a Roberto Benigni Film Festival would surely pump emotions. Benigni's leap-to-the-top-of-a-seat reaction to winning his first Oscar, for Best Foreign Language Film, is proof to newcomers of Benigni films that his work closely follows his personality by offering the unexpected. I admire this Italian actor and director with the courage to be silly, serious, striking—a man willing to play out his mind and express himself with gusto! The near-calamitous edge to his Oscar-winning film was both daring and brilliant.

Smitten by Benigni, I watched the entire Academy Awards held in 1999, a feat I'd never before accomplished. A few weeks prior to the awards, after reading that Roberto was scheduled for an appearance on *The Rosie O'Donnell Show*, I'd tuned in to catch Rosie presenting her guest with a hat that once belonged to Charlie Chaplin. (Benigni is a huge Chaplin fan.) Then, when the Oscar-winning Italian appeared on the *Late Show* shortly after awards night, I was there. I watched David Letterman struggle over what to do with Roberto, and I loved it! Loved that Roberto made the show host feel awkward. Since Letterman excels in prompting awkwardness in others, it was fun to see it turned all around.

It's also exciting to create video festivals for selected cities or regions, though some—Venice, Rome, Naples, or Tuscany and Sicily—are easier to visit on screen than others. The first three destinations are particularly plump with video options, and in recent years two R-rated films (*The Wings of the Dove* and *Dangerous Beauty*) have heightened period Venice offerings.

Since its release a few years ago, *The Wings of the Dove,* based on a Henry James novel and starring Helena Bonham Carter, offers a lusty contrast to my prized Venice favorite, *Summertime.* Hepburn and Carter are flagrant antitheses of each other, while the furnishings with reproduction Fortuny fabrics on the Venetian sets of *The Wings of the Dove* are a must-see extravaganza.

And with the unfurling of *Dangerous Beauty*, I've revamped my purely architectural perspective of sixteenth-century Venice. I'm now curious to learn about the real poet and courtesan of the times, Veronica Franco, a spirited prostitute with a courtly clientele, and the movie's heroine. Unfortunately, one of the film's alternate titles before its release, *Courtesan*, is more plot-revealing than the generic appellation it finally received. (Does someone actually get *paid* to give dumb titles to movies these days?) The movie, however, is saved by its poetic language. As in the films *Il Postino*, with its Dante lyrics, and *Much Ado About Nothing* and *A Midsummer Night's Dream* with their Shakespearean lines, poetry is the mainstay of *Dangerous Beauty*.

But where is the movie about Robert and Elizabeth Browning—my favorite Italy-loving poets? Where is the cinema saga I would title *Casa Guidi Windows* (based on Elizabeth Barrett Browning's poem of the same name)—a movie portraying Italy's *Risorgimento*, or struggle for political unity? Or why not a film that captures Casa Guidi (the Brownings' residence in Florence) as the center of a distinguished circle of notable writers: George Sand, Harriet Beecher Stowe, Nathaniel Hawthorne, George Eliot.

And where is the motion picture I'd name *The Englishman in Italy*, based on Robert Browning's poem of matching title? Ripe with depictions of land, sea, and life, his composition couldn't help but paint beautiful settings for a historical—or contemporary—Robert-and-Elizabeth story.

Instead, *The Barretts of Wimpole Street* is the title you'll find. It's the only movie I've discovered thus far that chronicles at least a portion of the lives of Elizabeth Barrett and Robert Browning, their meeting and courtship. Yet it ends with their matrimonial "escape" to Italy, their initial steps on Italian soil. So where's the sequel? Where's the story of the Brownings in Italy? Are there movies I've missed?

Perhaps for a start someone will snag screenplay rights to Margaret Forster's existing legend about the Brownings, her book *Lady's Maid*. Sewing together fact and fiction, Forster's pages offer greater detail than the simple life of Elizabeth's personal servant and companion. Yet I can only hope that the name would be changed to give viewers a hint of the movie's content—to let us know, ahead of time, that we're in for a poetic treat, partaking not only of Robert and Elizabeth's courtship through the eyes of Elizabeth's maid, but also later traveling with the Brownings in Italy.

CHAPTER FOUR

Learn to Speak a Little Italian

I f you're so crazy about Italy, then how come you haven't learned to speak Italian? David quizzed me, a few months before our September trip. "Don't worry," I said. "Someday I will."

How dare he remind me of something I'd postponed on purpose. Can I help that my *best* response to intimidation is procrastination? Besides, I had taken the first step. I'd placed it on a list. Long ago penciled between "clean out refrigerator" and "rotate tires—find warranty first," the words "learn to speak Italian" were scribbled on a pad.

If I were traveling alone I knew I'd be okay—I wouldn't mind embarrassing myself with the language. But making the journey with my husband was exhausting to think about.

David was counting on me for omnipotent communication the way a soothsayer is expected to predict the future.

It finally took an ultimatum. David threatened to back out on our anniversary tour if I didn't learn enough Italian to "get us by," as he called it. His better-learn-a-little-Italian threat scared me, but only because I realized how soon we were scheduled to leave. I wasn't really worried about David not going. He was always backing out—like the last time he said he wasn't going to Italy and he suggested someone else take his place: "Why don't you go with a friend, someone who likes to travel more than I do?"

But in a heartbeat I'd replied, "Oh, no. You're not going to have that to hang over my head later on. I'm not about to take somebody else on *our* twentieth anniversary trip. I'll simply save your ticket and go twice!"

It was an answer he hadn't expected.

The countdown had started and panic set in. Three weeks to go, and *still*, I could only spit out a few foreign words: the equivalent of hello, thank you, excuse me, a couple of numbers, occasional food items—not much considering a nine-month notice of impending travel.

Sure, I'd watched scores of subtitled Italian-language movies, listened to dozens of opera recordings, and sung along with contemporary Italian singers. But why had I postponed the sensible course of action? Avoided the obvious solution of immersing myself in a formal language course?

Now, it was out of the question. I'd waited too late. My only option at this point was to sign up for a *mini*-class and face the scores of phrase books and dictionaries gathering dust on my "Italian language" bookshelf. My longtime friend, procrastination, now turned her back to me and laughed, pretending to be a stranger.

Almost from the start, upon quickly discovering that learning a language is predictable in one sure-fire way, I nearly gave up. Why is it that the one word you wish to decipher can never be found without digging? Why, in a bilingual ruse of hide-and-seek, do editors persist in obscuring the very words you're looking for?

Translation? Words that can't be located in one dictionary may be found in another, or in a third, fourth, or fifth source. Or they may never be found at all. Far worse, a word's meaning in one region often varies from its meaning in another—something a Type-A and over-forty personality can't handle. The imprecision, to my eyes, involved in comparing one language to another makes me crazy. I want Italian to function like English, and my brain balks, freezing like the cursor on my computer during crashes, when it doesn't work that way—when word-for-word comparisons don't automatically exist for my convenience.

Then, after organizing and shuffling through dictionaries—a procrastinator cleaning her closet—it was time for a blackboard. My first teacher, Mrs. Griggs, had produced magical "foreign" words for me on her blackboard when I was in first grade, so I followed her example.

As prominently displayed as my map of Italy, my little oak-framed blackboard made eye contact with me every time I walked by—a portrait following me with dusty eyes. I chalked new words and phrases and repeated old ones. We talked to each other like roommates, discussing train schedules and directions of travel, times of day and days of the week.

Sticking stickers soon followed. Like a toddler proud of a new trick, I peeled labels from a workbook and stuck them on everything. In our upstairs private bathroom (where guests wouldn't have to read before peeing), I tagged all the basic equipment. On the toilet tank I stuck *gabinetto*; where the shower curtain meets the tile wall I placed *doccia*; on the bathtub skirt I adhered *vasca da bagno*; the sink backsplash received *lavandino*; and a mirror was labeled *specchio*.

After stickers, I flashed cards. My friend Ali suggested I make a custom set—giant cards, big enough to read while walking. I liked the idea from the start. Since Texans talk different than the words described in phrase books (at least I do), I would carve my own niche in Italian. I'd create my own mix of words, a Texan-Italian lexicon to accompany my southern accent. After all, I was doomed to be a "Texan in Tuscany" as soon as I opened my mouth.

Ali even offered to "flash" with me on the hike-and-bike trail along the Colorado River that runs through Austin. While others walked their dogs, pushed baby strollers, or jogged, we quizzed one another in Italian—repeating the names of foods, asking each other how to buy groceries in an *alimentari*. We practiced how to take a bus downtown: *Dov'è l'autobus per il centro città, per favore?*

My final learning strategy was straightforward. In desperation, I listened to audiocassettes during the near nine-hour flight to Italy. By the time the plane landed at Milan's Malpensa airport, I was dizzy with jumbled foreign words and last-minute attempts at conjugation. Yet despite my efforts, it wasn't enough; my mind turned as limp as spaghetti. A big fat nothing came rolling into my head as I walked the corridors toward emigration. Instead of saying *buon giorno* to the official who asked to see my passport, I responded with a mouse-like "hello."

On foreign soil, everything flip-flopped. When I knew the right words to say in Italian, the Italians I was with spoke English with pride. I didn't have the courage to ask them to "help" me by speaking the local language. Then when every foreign word I'd ever learned left my brain, no one spoke English at all. And they zoomed through their words like tapes on fast forward.

David's pre-trip enthusiasm for learning Italian was *subtle*. He learned one word. But he *is* proof that you don't need many words to communicate in Italy.

Before leaving, David found out the Italian expression for bicycle, *bicicletta*, more so to recognize it on a sign than to say it. After arriving in Italy, however, my husband quickly added four items to his word stash. In La Spezia, he learned to say "barn jarno," the Texan farm version of *buon giorno*. By the time we arrived in Siena, he'd picked up "gratsee, gratsee" on the train and started thanking everybody for everything twice. Then in Vicenza, David memorized *prosciutto* and *panini* so he could order ham sandwiches on his own after riding a bicycle all morning. Stubbornly avoiding the singular form, *panino,* even after I'd tried to explain the difference, he concluded, "It doesn't matter what I really say as long as I raise one or two fingers to indicate the number of sandwiches I want."

A word here and there was enough. Through David's lips, I heard a partial reincarnation of Mark Twain's words from his essay, "Italian Without a Master."

> The "help" are all natives; they talk Italian to me, I answer in English; I do not understand them, they do not understand me, consequently no harm is done, and everybody is satisfied. In order to be just and fair, I throw in an Italian word when I have one, and this has a good influence.

When I tried to explain the difference between *prosciutto cotto* (cooked ham) and *prosciutto crudo* (salt- and air-cured ham), David likewise waved me off saying it didn't matter. And it didn't. Butchers in Italy seem to know that Texans prefer their food to be cooked.

David's favorite words to say were *due acqua naturale*. Right away, at a pizzeria or *trattoria*, he'd order two big bottles of water while I puzzled with the menu. After holding up two fingers (in case the waiter missed the *due* part), he'd also indicate the desired bottle size with the height of his hand above the table. I knew David well enough to realize he was ordering in defense, ordering extra water up front.

When I read that Italians have a different way of counting with their fingers, I decided to master the technique. It would be a subtle talent, but I needed a good confidence-booster. Self-scheduled as I was to be speaking recognizable Italian by the year 2009 (according to current progress), I welcomed a lesser challenge.

It's my understanding that counting in Italian goes something like this. Pointing a thumb up in the air indicates the number one (as opposed to Americans using their index finger), and for two, the index finger is added. The middle digit goes up for three, four fingers without the thumb makes four, and a spread-eagled hand is five.

The simplicity of the foreign method intrigued me as I embraced the notion of counting with my fingers once again. It reminded me of how I used to mimic my father when he counted livestock with his hands when I was a child. His technique was more visual. Two counts at a time—double fingers on one hand flicking in rhythm with each pair of cows, sheep, or goats—checking to see if the right number of animals made it in or out of a pen or pasture.

Uno, due, tre, quattro, cinque, and I'm back to practicing finger numbers in Italian, one through five. But I'm alarmed when I stick up *uno* and *due* alone (pointing my thumb and index finger) for I feel like I'm robbing a bank. Can this be right? I start worrying about the prospect of asking for two kilos of fruit at a *fruttivendolo.* Will they throw grapes across the counter at me and then stick their hands up in the air?

Traveling alone to Italy is easy. Explaining *why* you traveled alone is more difficult. Last year, I finally dove headfirst from the high board, without a buddy or companion as a life jacket. I was anxious to test the *new* language, my few skinny words of Italian.

But my immediate task was to work on this book. This trip was *business.*

Yeah, right. Every time I mentioned to friends that I

was going to Italy on business, they laughed. "Does your venture need a new partner? Can I go to Italy too?"

Deciding to stop taking paying clients had been difficult. After six exciting but exhaustive years working for the state on a huge preservation and restoration project of the Texas Capitol, I was enjoying self-employment again. Combined with design work, historic preservation research and consulting kept me busy. Yet the urge to write about Italy kept festering within me, growling like an empty stomach. By the time David and I celebrated our twentieth anniversary, it had developed into a blown-out fever. So here I was back in Italy, the following year, on a sixteen-day writing journey to the Veneto and Tuscany regions—a cheap writer's tour, mostly one-star hotels.

This time, with only myself to amuse, I let Italy happen on its own. No minimum number of museums and historical sites to check off each day. No exhaustive itinerary to keep pace with. Except for a few literary outings I'd planned— tracking the previous footsteps of noteworthy writers, I wanted to see where the "language" would take me.

Immersing full body and soul, I was hoping my brain would absorb the foreign words I was too lazy to learn back home. I'd soak up the dialect and return to Texas rolling my r's with worldly zest. Two weeks of taking in the flowing words of Italy and I'd exchange my Texas drawl for a Latin-based cadence.

Or so I'd predicted.

The reality of the situation proved more like a flea-market find, elusive and predictably fake. Never able to procure the authentic, I picked up near words instead, words and syllables reeking of rip-off artist and chicanery. Even when I repeated phrases immediately after hearing them, something was lost in the translation, garbled between teeth and tongue. What my ears took in and my mouth spat out were closer to distant cousins than recognizable twins. My attempt at digesting Italian firsthand was a regurgitated disaster.

It only took a few days in Italy before I revised my expectations. In lieu of expecting to devour the language, I settled for nibbled bits. Fresh words through osmosis were welcomed with awe. (Where did I pick up *that* phrase?) But my new plan of action was to implement the old, the skimpy vocabulary I'd supposedly memorized before leaving home.

For starters, there was bed and bath terminology to contend with. My greatest bathroom-challenged accommodations were in Venice. I'd not booked early enough and was not spending enough buckets of *lire* to get a room on a canal, but I was close. The tiny *albergo* fronted on a quiet street of water.

Reminiscent of a college dormitory room, my Venetian cubicle was surprisingly cheerful. Predictably peaceful, its green-shuttered window peeked out onto a tiny courtyard of inactivity. But the bath situation (always a surprise in Italy) was less obvious. Nothing looked like my sticker-clad objects at home!

The first thing to catch my eye was a plastic, one-piece, mini-bidet you could move around the room. It came equipped with its own plastic cup for carrying water from the *lavandino* near the window. Did I *need* to move the bidet about the room? Should I move it to the window and toss any dirty water outside? Or should I pour dirty water down the only drain in sight, the basin where I'd wash my hair and brush my teeth?

Then, above the sink, catching my reflection in a mirror, I instantly realized I'd wasted precious mental real estate by memorizing the word for a "looking glass," *specchio*. I could think of no reason now or ever to talk about this mirror or any other.

And when I finally found the toilet, the label on the door was simply *toilette*, not the strange *gabinetto* word that was stuck on my white ceramic tank back in Austin.

But the real challenge in my bed and bath situation had nothing to do with words in any language. It dealt with location and distance, physical attributes rather than appellations. My bed was on the third floor; the *toilette* was on the fourth floor; the *bagno* (spelled like the sticker on my tub at home!) was on the second floor; and if you wanted a *doccia*, or shower, it was on floor number one. Like guessing the winning door in a game show.

Booking a vacant room in Venice in early May had been tougher than anticipated. Somewhere between faxing and calling a dozen *alberghi*, I'd forgotten my nightly routine—my habitual rising five times a night. I'd forgotten to ask, "How far to the toilet?"

With a pillow providing the comfort of a rock, I passed a restless first night in Venice. When I finally inspected the so-called pillow's hard inner core, I found it to be upholstered, tufted with buttons like a sofa. No amount of fluffing was going to soften its form.

Blessings, however, often arrive in circuitous ways. During one of my fidgety jaunts upstairs that night, I passed by a balcony where you could hear a midnight *gondoliere* singing a wistful tune. Opening a pair of arch-top glass doors, I stepped onto a tiny stone ledge—a balcony barely large enough for my feet and one pot of red geraniums (the national balcony flower of Italy!). The canvas before me was painted with romance. A full moon cast its glow upon the passing gondola with its lullaby-singing guide and clinging lovers, tourists in love, with each other or with Venice. It was one of those moments you dream about but don't expect to come true.

Once the gondola passed, I listened for a moment to the clicking sound of footsteps on stone, a sole pedestrian down the narrow alley below me. Then I climbed a double flight of stairs to rumble the building with an ungentle flush of the *toilette*. Tiptoeing downstairs again, I returned to my rock of Gibraltar, my pillow of Carrara marble. I dreamed of moon-filled gondolas with serenaded strangers and of shadows bouncing back and forth along canals, *palazzo* to *palazzo*. Finally, gently stirred to a rising dawn by pebble music on glass, I dug out my Italian dictionary and looked up the word for rain—*pioggia*.

Savor the Food and Drink of Regional Italy

S everal years ago, when David first asked me what Italian restaurants were like during my first trip abroad, I laughed and said, "I don't know. I never ate in one." I'd only eaten *one* sit-down meal during my entire stay in Italy, and even then the food was ordered for me.

It was during a summer of architectural study in 1988 that my friend Linda and I were asked to dine at a remote little establishment outside Vicenza. Our host was a wealthy businessman we'd met on the train from Milan earlier in the day, a native Vicenzan. After he and his wife picked us up at our hotel in a big Mercedes-Benz, we drove through the *campagna* to a *ristorante* that was open in the middle of August vacation—a time when most eating places were closed.

More precisely, we raced, without limit or apparent control. The steel-blue sedan followed its path of choice: an invisible racetrack down the middle of a winding road. Curves were banked with screeching brakes applied at the last moment, almost as an afterthought. Then, with eyebrows cocked in amazement, Linda and I shot glances at each other when we flew past the famous Villa Rotonda—Andrea Palladio's architectural grand dame. The Palladian villa was one reason for our coming to Vicenza in the first place, and its regal prominence on a hill was more captivating, more dramatic than we'd ever imagined.

My first experience with the driving habits of Italians, combined with the unexpected siting of the Villa Rotonda, left me speechless. But not for long. There was more.

The Mercedes excursion past Palladio's masterpiece was satisfaction enough for lovers of Renaissance architecture like us, but the evening kept getting better. We next stopped at the "house" of our host's brother to visit with family members and share *antipasti* in prelude to an evening of dining. Again, Linda and I stole looks and then whispered to each other. "Can you believe all of this?" I said, spotting vineyards as we pulled into a crushed-granite driveway. "Do you think this place *really* belongs to his brother?"

"I don't know, but this is no house," Linda replied. "It's a villa!"

Our native acquaintance soon offered the details. "We'll stop for a moment and you can meet my brother. He and his wife are joining us for dinner. And, in case you're curious, my brother's place is quite old. It's a country villa constructed several centuries ago and reputedly designed by Scamozzi. Simple, but nice, don't you think? Being architecture students, I thought you might like it."

"Yes, yes. It's *wonderful*," we said, chiming in unison like singing canaries. Then also simultaneously, we reached for our cameras—equipment that didn't exist! In a flash, we realized we'd committed the ultimate photographer's sin. In response to our exhaustion from the overnight train from Barcelona, and utterly thankful for the invitation to dinner our first night in Italy, we'd both hidden our cameras in the hotel room. Something we'd never done before! We were going to eat. What was the point in taking cameras when soon it would be dark?

Wrong. Now, we'd never have proof of our incredulous adventure.

Following formal introductions, Linda and I were led to an orchard behind the main structure and asked to pick a couple of pears to accompany a simple *antipasto*—local wine and cheese with pick-your-own fruit. Back inside the cool stone walls, however, our four eyes absorbed everything—each architectural and furnishings detail in sight. While we poured admirations and gulped "architecture," our hosts poured and drank vintage wine.

Later at the restaurant, we were further entertained as endless courses of steaming dishes, along with a special olive oil, were ordered and presented for the entire table— a deed I was thankful for. Though incredibly, I don't remember eating. Instead I was entranced, enchanted by the presence of folk music. Four brothers from a nearby *fattoria*, or farm, were dining and singing in the next room. Round after round, the *fratelli* warbled regional ballads and swigged local wine—scenes and sounds I committed to memory.

Peanut butter. We ran out of peanut butter in Florence. "What now?" I asked Linda, knowing our food budget was nonexistent. While we were happy and satisfied devouring buildings, not pasta, losing our favorite accompaniment to bread was alarming.

Our decision to take peanut butter that summer had been a good one. In England and France, we'd routinely stashed our hard morning rolls to make peanut butter sandwiches for the day. But now, only a few days into Italy, our last jar of sticky sustenance had been depleted.

"It won't be Jif or Skippy, but surely there's some kind of peanut butter in one of these markets," I said, as we walked inside the first of several *alimentari*, or grocery shops, before succeeding in our quest.

"But what about all that fresh pasta and pizza?" gourmet-loving friends later asked me, trying to understand why we'd taken our own food. "How could you pass on the chance to eat fresh ravioli and fettuccine? How could you ignore the pizza?"

But the answer was easy: "I always knew I'd go back."

Since the words "food" and "Italy" are synonymous for most people, I understood their disbelief—not eating local cuisine *was* sinful. But for Linda and me, at the time, architecture was the source of all cravings. We were young and living the Latin phrase: "eating to live, not living to eat."

Unfortunately, David's and my anniversary trip to Italy warranted more food expertise than pointing to a flavor of ice cream (something I could do blindfolded already). This trip was my idea, my responsibility. It was critical that I learn how to order in restaurants with a degree of confidence. Local dishes. I knew navigating an Italian menu could be like squeezing an orange and getting lemonade. So perhaps more than anything else, I wanted to avoid the ultimate foreign-language calamity. Skirt the ubiquitous faux pas of saying something stupid and never knowing it (except by the waiter's expression). Exposing my inadequacies in public by ordering a *pesca* instead of *pesce* (peach instead of fish), *fragole* instead of *fagioli*

(strawberries instead of beans), or *peperoni* (sweet peppers) when David wanted pepperoni sausage on his pizza, held little attraction for me. And what if I said something worse? Something surly or dirty!

One of the greatest pleasures of Italian cuisine is reading and contemplating it beforehand. And learning about Italian food and cooking means concentrating on regional character—forgetting about Italy as a whole.

The country is deceivingly young, with less than one and a half centuries of political unity. (The country became unified about the time of our Civil War.) Yet people outside Italy steadfastly refer to everything in Italy as "Italian"; I too am guilty. But Italians are fiercely provincial. Foods, like the people and the products they produce, are Tuscan, Ligurian, or Sicilian—not simply "Italian." Expecting to find a particular region's famous dish throughout the country is, therefore, insulting. Guaranteeing distinction and freshness, each region cooks with local products and with produce in season—cooking that makes sense.

But learning about Italian dining is more than interpreting regional differences. It's also about learning how to take things *slow* and *easy*, letting food arrive without worry—eating when the food is ready, not simply when you want to eat. Since the Piedmont region's instigation of a "slow-food" movement in the 1980s (a reaction to the McDonald's invasion), it seems ridiculous to think in terms of fast food in Italy when many restaurants proudly display the symbol for Slow Food International—a snail. In a setting where dishes are typically not cooked until ordered, what sense does it make to act all-American and hurried?

But David didn't see it that way.

"Try to relax and enjoy the moment," I whispered to him one evening in Siena. "What's your hurry?"

I was hoping he'd warm to clock-stopping meals the way I had, but was I expecting too much too soon? Were a few days in Italy sufficient time to change the well-worn habits of my husband? A man who clutches a salt shaker in anticipation of dousing his plate before tasting. Who routinely instructs waiters to leave the check at the same time they bring out the food. Who is guilty in Texas restaurants of wiring a transistor radio to one ear to hear updated baseball scores.

Even with a spouse who claims that "leisurely dining" is an oxymoron, my experiences with David in Italy were rewarding and revealing. When the two of us relished our first Italian meal, *real* pizza in a La Spezia pizzeria, we realized that pizza pies don't come pre-sliced to the table and the locals don't eat pizza with their hands. (How crude we were in Texas!) As if eating veal cutlets or sirloin steak, diners in La Spezia ate their pizza with a fork and knife. Needless to say, we likewise ate *our* pizza with utensils, hoping to diminish our Texan profile. Only later did we notice that when buying "day" pizza by the *pezzo*, or piece, usually stand-up or take-out, it's okay to eat pizza with your hands—the same way, I've been told, that pizza is often eaten in southern Italy.

Other dining moments were also revealing.

On another evening, in Siena, our third night in a row to dine at the same *ristorante* (David's "if-it's-good-why-go-some-place-new" philosophy), we splurged on a multi-course meal. Or at least I did. David had his usual *funghi* and *prosciutto* pizza. Sitting at the same table as on previous nights (another high-ranking habit according to "The Fine Art of Dining" by David), we settled into the rhythm of Sienese cuisine.

A shared *antipasto* came first: *salumi* with fresh figs. But bread was David's primary target while waiting on his pizza—basket after basket of crusty, rustic chunks that he doused with a local olive oil, *olio extra vergine d'oliva*. Skipping the *primo* (typically pasta), I proceeded to the *secondo*, requesting *vitello*, or veal. And at the same time I ordered a *contorno*, a side dish of zucchini in this case. We never made it to the *dolci*, the sweet treats of Italy that must have surely inspired the familiar saying: "Eat pie first." Instead, like buzzards clothespinned to a fence and waiting for road kill, we coveted every other diner's desert as it spun into view on the kitchen's tiered and revolving server. Each stunning *piatto*, or dish, enticed more than the one before it. David, however, never accepted the Italian order of things, never warmed to the notion that my vegetable would come out last.

"Let me get the waiter," he said, trying to be helpful. "I'm sure they forgot your zucchini."

"But they didn't forget." And I paused. "That's why it's called *courses*. That's how it works in Italy."

Then calmly, David added, "And you wonder why I always order pizza."

Obviously, one trip was not enough. One visit to Italy would never suffice in altering David's mind to accept "slow food." My husband's transition to *la dolce vita* would require another journey.

Among other things, I collect bottles. The shapes and colors of Italian bottled waters, sodas, beers, wines, and spirits intrigue me. Tracking their sources of origin takes me to new regions—unfamiliar destinations to better learn the land I love. Reading the fine print on labels to identify source cities, or locales, I then circle the locations on my wall map and scribble side notes in the margins. For bottled waters I circle San Pellegrino near Bergamo (San Pellegrino®), Adamello-Brenta Protected National Park and Carisolo (Surgiva®), Scarperia (Panna®-San Pellegino®), and Nuvolento (Solé™), among others.

More than a year ago, I called all the specialty and gourmet grocers in Austin.

"Hello. I'm a writer working on a book about Italy, and I'm trying to identify all the products you carry that are imported from there. Do you have a list?" (I live by lists!)

"No, I'm afraid not. We buy from a number of distributors, and there's never been a reason for us to keep track that way." So I'm back to scanning grocery shelves and reading labels.

My cronies find this sad, but because it's such a rare occasion that I ever taste or drink wine, reading labels on bottles provides the only clues I have for evaluating the contents. Out of worry over selecting the wrong thing (or being ill advised) for Italian dinner parties, I sometimes even suggest to close friends that they bring their own—a wine from Italy so I can add another empty bottle to my collection. Consequently, I offer no expertise with wine except to direct you to resources discovered through research and discussions with friends.

A perennial favorite reference appears to be Victor Hazan's *Italian Wine* (1982), according to reliable sources—the dear friends who save bottles for me. The format of Marc and Kim Millon's guidebook *The Wine Roads of Italy* (1991) appears to be helpful in the way it pairs the wine with the land. And I'm lured by the graphic layout of *Touring in Wine Country: Tuscany* (1996), by Maureen Ashley; its photos and illustrations seduce whether you drink wine or not.

For my own quirky beverage in lieu of wine, I buy bottles of pomegranate juice and Italian sparkling water to make a nonalcoholic version of a drink I once read about called *tintoretto*—made with pomegranate juice and Prosecco wine (a popular wine of the Veneto, typically sparkling). I mix equal parts juice and water and then lapse in the "pomegranate days" of my childhood. Luring me with their waterlogged seeds bursting through scarlet skin, pomegranates signaled the closing of summer. Never having seen the red fruit in a grocery store as a child, I instead picked them from old shrubs that were still growing on my grandaddy's place, botanical vestiges of a former homestead.

Now, pomegranates remind me of Italy.

From another direction, Ernest Hemingway reminds me of Italy. He taught me a lot about drinking! I once entered a contest: The Harry's Bar and American Grill International Imitation Hemingway Competition, sponsored by PEN Center USA West. Though I didn't win a prize, the experience of entering the contest was worth it.

The competition headline seduced me. It went something like this: "Once again, write one really good page of really bad Hemingway and it could land you and a friend in Italy." Reeled in by the "Italy" word, I dug out a few Hemingway titles, some I'd read before but didn't remember. Although the contest promised dinner for two at Harry's Bar & American Grill in Florence, *Across the*

River and Into the Trees provided insight into Harry's Bar in Venice, the original location. And it was in this book that I discovered Italian firewater, a high-octane product called grappa. Curious, I was prompted to then read about Bassano de Grappa, the quaint medieval town with its famous covered bridge, north of Padua. Famous for its grappa production, it's another tiny circle on my wall map.

Dining in Italy is an athletic event of considerable duration, both slow in pace and full of action. And at home, *la cucina* is the genius loci, the center of activity for *famiglia* and *amici*, family and friends. Whether Italians are dining out or eating in, noon or night, their clocks stop ticking for meals.

When I planned our anniversary vacation in Italy, I knew David would either love it or hate it. Thumbs up or thumbs down, like a Roman emperor signaling a gladiator's fate.

I worried. Will he embrace the old buildings as much as I do? Will he welcome riding the trains in Italy—his first train experience ever? Will the bathrooms meet his standard of cleanliness? Such questions made my head throb; the fretting made me queasy. My heart longed for Italy, and I was dragging my husband there with me like a puppy on a leash.

The food did it. I shouldn't have worried so much. David fell in love with Italy amidst pizza crumbs, *prosciutto* smells, pasta swirlings, and gelati drippings. The architecture was spectacular. Trains were easy except on one occasion in Florence. And though the bathrooms were weird, they were exceedingly clean, and outfitted with starched and ironed toweling. But the food surpassed all else.

I've never cooked with Marcella Hazan, but I did the next best thing. I took a cooking class a few years ago with her son, Giuliano Hazan. It turned out to be a wonderful experience, not just because of the sumptuous dishes that were prepared and sampled but because Giuliano's presence made Marcella come alive. She was real, a person beyond the images in the cookbooks on my shelves.

I remember how, just as the Blanco River flowed beyond the open kitchen windows of a cooking school (now closed) in Wimberley, Texas, my thoughts drifted during Giuliano's culinary performance. While he fielded questions pertaining to ingredients and preparation techniques, I focused on a single thought, a question I knew I'd never ask: What was it *really* like to grow up in a kitchen with Marcella?

More recently, I attended another cooking class with Hazan. This time it was at a new cooking school in

Fredericksburg, Texas. It's the same little town in the Texas Hill Country where last year David and I bought a small house, for use as a bicycling getaway for him and writing retreat for me. So you can imagine how excited I was to have Giuliano Hazan give a cooking class practically in my own back yard. The next time, however, I hope it's in Italy, attending one of his sessions in the Veneto. And I'll ask him to autograph his newest cookbook, *Every Night Italian*, to accompany my (already signed) copy of his step-by-step masterpiece, *The Classic Pasta Cookbook* (1993).

For the times when I can't find (or afford) a current cooking class, I buy a new, or new-to-me used cookbook instead. Marcella Hazan's hefty cookbook called *Marcella Cucina* (1997) was purchased the moment it hit bookstore shelves. And a real treasure-trove was Faith Willinger's *Red, White and Greens: The Italian Way with Vegetables* (1996); I found it for half price at a used bookstore. David knows my weakness too. Last Christmas, he surprised me with another dandy, *Sophia Loren's Recipes and Memories* (1998). Filled with more than recipes, it's loaded with film facts, early photos of the actress, and clipped movie images, many with co-star Marcello Mastroianni.

And what about out-of-print cookbooks? I find a certain attraction in locating something that's not easy to find. Perhaps it's the detective in me. (I wanted to be an FBI agent when I was in fifth grade.) How easy it now is to locate old cookbooks through book searches, using local or on-line bookseller services, or by doing it yourself. The downside to cookbook and other book searches on the Internet, however, is the "loss of the thrill." It's still more exciting to spot a much-sought-after old book on a dusty bookshelf, more "detective-like" to discover a crinkled and torn book jacket and find lost notes tucked inside.

A few years ago I conducted multiple on-line searches in hopes of locating a copy of Elizabeth David's *Italian Food* (originally published in 1954), a book I'd pined over for years. I was surprised to finally locate a hardcover copy at a reasonable price. Since I had seen only original and 1987 editions in libraries, I'd expected a "rare book" situation, meaning a high price. But it wasn't. Of course, shortly after receiving my *proud* purchase in the mail, I understood why the price was so low. Evidently, the book had been re-released for a *third* time, in 1996. My sought-after tome was *less* obscure than I'd first imagined, and my investigative skills were now questionable. Within a week of my purchase, I even noticed multiple copies of the 1996 edition in a local bookstore. Still, I treasure my "hard-to-get" copy of Elizabeth David's *Italian Food*. Pining and searching as I did, over time, had made it more precious than ever.

Equal parts memoir and recipes, two more cookbooks (included in Books That Depict Italy) are special to me. The seasonal entries of Elizabeth Romer's *The Tuscan Year: Life and Food in an Italian Valley* remind me of my own youthful experiences on a farm in Central Texas:

gardening and raising cows, sheep, goats, pigs, and chickens. And in Maria Grammatico and Mary Taylor Simeti's *Bitter Almonds: Recollections and Recipes from a Sicilian Girlhood* is where I located the recipe for the first biscotti I ever made. My initial encounter with making the slender, crisp biscuits was also memorable because it was so easy—so easy that biscotti bakings provided all my baked Christmas gifts that year.

Further influencing my Italy-loving habits are the Italian-cooking chefs on TV. As often as possible, I time meal breaks to coincide with (sometimes available) favorite shows: *Bugialli's Italy* (hosted by Giuliano Bugialli), *Lidia's Italian Table* (hosted by Lidia Bastianich), and *Molto Mario* (hosted by Mario Batali). Unfortunately, after The Learning Channel dropped its cooking shows a while back, watching Biba Caggiano in *Biba's Italian Kitchen* was no longer an option. And since my cable service no longer carries Mary Ann Esposito's *Ciao Italia* or Nick Stellino's *CucinaAmore* (I miss his kiss-tossing "mama mias"!), my choices have been further reduced.

Wherever your mania lies with food or drink, let it lead. If cooking is your passion, investigate the breadth of possibilities with regionally inspired cooking classes. Learn the hundreds of pasta shapes by name.

If Tuscany is your dream destination, create a Tuscan-style picnic at home. Outfit a basket with the gastronomical accoutrements of Italian hill towns, and dine alfresco on a make-believe outing.

If it's truffles that interest you, learn all you can about *tartufi bianchi d'Alba*, the famous light-colored but highly perfumed truffles of Alba, the white truffle capital of Italy in the Piedmont region. Capture the truffle-seasoned explorations of Jeffery Steingarten's appetizing essay, "Hail Cesare," in his 1997 gluttonous concoction, *The Man Who Ate Everything*. Follow Steingarten as he learns the truffle-buying secrets of a celebrated chef and the secrets of a professional truffle hunter—a *trifulau*. Then read Michael Dibdin's wine-and-dine mystery titled *A Long Finish* to digest the obsessive mortal value of "white diamonds."

Or, if it's wine, study everything you can about Italian offerings. Develop an expertise from your passion. Be zealous. From *uva* to *cantina* to *tavola*, grapes to cellar to table, practice the vocabulary of *vitocoltura*. Push beyond ordinary knowledge to memorize some of the native red, or dark, grape varieties—Nebbiolo, Sangiovese, Barbera, Dolcetto, Schiava, Corvina, and Montepulciano. Impress your friends. Retain the names of several native white, or light, grapes—Garganega, Trebbiano, Cortese, Traminer, and a few nonnative white varieties—Pinot Bianco, Pinot Grigio, and Riesling. Impress yourself. Examine the various groups of sweet wines, such as Moscato Bianco and

Moscato Giallo, made with white and yellow muscat grapes. Then wallow in your knowledge.

Master the vocabulary of producing and tasting wine. Fantasize about the *vendemmia* (grape harvest), *feste* and *sagre* (festivals), and Italian *enoteche*—wine "libraries" where regional or national wines can be sampled and purchased in Italy. Try new-to-you wines while dining and by attending local wine tastings at home. Peruse rows of bottles in wine shop aisles and study guidebooks to expand your ability to connect the various grapes and blends with resulting wines and their appropriate regions.

From *vino da tavola*, or unclassified table wine, to bottles with appellation, Italian wines are worthy of obsessing over and collecting—even if, like me, your collection is one of empty bottles salvaged from trash cans and begged from friends.

Keep a Notebook, Journal, or "Scrapbox"

The best way to remember something is to write it down. I use notebooks and an Italian pen! Little pieces of paper get lost or misplaced. I discover them years later in the Christmas wrapping drawer or in a cookbook marking a recipe I once tried. Unfettered notes never make it to the stack or file for which they were intended. No better than messages written with invisible ink, they fly around the house to land where I can never find them. Sometimes I think the dog chews them up, but since we *still* don't have a dog, he's invisible too.

For instant note-taking, buying my little flip-top notepad with refillable inserts was the best thing I'd done in years. It slips easily into my pocket or purse and I cram it full of notes-on-the-go: new and old book titles discovered while traveling, new-to-me places in Italy where friends have traveled, a new Italian restaurant for the next time I go to New York, Chicago, or San Francisco, the name of a cooking school in Florence, an upcoming opera spotted in *The New York Times,* or a promising new Web site with an Italian connection.

Periodically, I transfer my tiny field notes to spiral-bound notebooks and manila folders at home. I buy cheap notebooks, half the size of a regular sheet of paper, six at a time so I never run out. Finicky about organization, I separate the material into categories: I jot movie and book titles in one notebook, food and dining references in another, travel facts or potential destinations in a third, *ad infinitum.* Sometimes I color code or collage the covers and label them with titles that tickle the tongue: Italian Food Fantasies (decadent recipes and food origins) or Vines, Wines, and Dines (romantic vineyard and restaurant destinations).

If spiral notebooks don't inspire you to write and keep notes about Italy, buy blank books instead. But don't do as I did. Don't buy a *first* blank book so fancy you're afraid to use it! I made that mistake in Venice long ago.

Beguiled by the artistry of handmade papers (so many to choose from!), I relinquished my credit card for an elegant, pristine volume with a blue-marble covering, a book bound by a strip of blue leather and clasped with brass fittings. Justifying the extravagance of a frivolous purchase (within the context of my peanut-butter existence), I told myself, "It will last a lifetime." The perfect blank canvas for my written dreams. A place for painting with words my inaugural Italian experiences.

But it never happened.

More than a decade later, my first blank book's virtue remains intact. I'm *still* saving it for a special occasion! Like an old maid on my shelf, my charming blank beauty from Venice is destined to remain a virgin for life. Each passing year makes her innocence more precious.

More recently, my husband has given me two leather journals, each handsome and handmade in Italy. Though I reserve them for noted events and treat them like fruit that will bruise, at least I write words on their pages. Like a pianist poised for performance, I pick up a writing stylus from Italy and strike first chords of my own.

My leather books record that which is precious to me: wedding anniversaries (what David and I did or didn't do that year); major changes in our lives (a new career or a move to a different house); special memories of family events, holidays, and birthdays; the titles of books I've read in a year; lofty inspirations of living in Italy (for six months? for a year?).

I recently read what I had inscribed on the inside cover of the first journal I received: "On the occasion of my for- tieth birthday . . . a present from David this Tuesday evening." And on the first page: "A co-worker gave me flowers early this morning before dashing off to the Capitol to take care of last-minute details regarding Governor Bush's inauguration. Yes, today is the day we embrace a new leader for the State of Texas! A large crowd gathered on the south lawn and . . ." While the writing wasn't as exciting as the cannon blasts that day, it froze a special time in my life.

But now guilt sets in, for I haven't revealed all. I shouldn't be bragging about writing in leather books, making it sound glamorous and romantic when it's not. At least it's less fanciful than I've led you to believe. In lieu of penning bold words in permanent ink (with a sleek Italian pen as I do with note cards and letters), I confess. I write with a pencil instead. A low-life piece of graphite. I still find it impossible to mar beautiful chaste pages with words that can't be erased!

They say daily "journaling" is a good way to get words on paper, but I've never been able to do it with ease. Daily writing for me is unpredictable: it's either painful like going to the dentist (something to be postponed), or it's like skipping and singing a song (difficult to keep inside).

More often than not, I scribble tiny stories at random—on pages where ink doesn't scare me. I post scattered anecdotes, funny-to-me or odd things that happen, or telling thoughts about David and me. It was in one of my notebooks in service a few years ago that I first noted the overwhelming and scary thought of traveling in Italy with my spouse. Envisioning David with all his luggage and bicycle gear, I wrote the simple words: "Rolling Across Italy" and "Life in the Baggage Lane." They were the seeds that sprouted this book.

"I have not sought to adorn my work with long phrases or high-sounding words," wrote Niccolò Machiavelli in *The Prince*, words that inspire me today. I find my best journal writing, my best thoughts about spirit and soul, to be nothing more than good exercise for dumping one's mind, a method for purging the brain of wordy clutter. I praise writer Natalie Goldberg for her writing suggestions in *Writing Down the Bones*, and Julia Cameron for the writing technique she calls "morning pages" in *The Artist's Way*. Both are fertile gardens for writers at any level. So even if you've never thought of yourself as a writer, digging through these resources with Italy in mind is a rewarding and comforting task.

Pre-trip writing pumps energy into my passion, keeps me inflated for times when I'm able to pack a bag. Whenever I read a book about the recording techniques of others, even a chapter or two, I'm motivated right away to chronicle new thoughts about Italy. And I've picked up helpful tips for making real travel writing more intimate: 1) don't expect your journal to be a precise record of every event, 2) describe in detail only that which interests you the most, and 3) don't worry about neatness and sentence structure. In other words, write from your heart, and don't think—famous advice from a number of wordsmiths! Pen your passions on paper and see where it takes you. To a deeper place? To the spot where your spirit is soothed?

Knowing my own limitations, I'm amazed how some individuals are well disciplined in keeping a notebook or journal, while others are not. How is it that writing and sketching in margins comes easy for one person and not another?

Michael J. Gelb, author of *How to Think like Leonardo da Vinci*, writes about how the famous artist utilized his notebooks to explore and record his natural curiosities. (I should be so curious!) Intermixing sketches, observations, and musings on various topics, Leonardo's notebooks were works of art for the eyes and mind. According to Gelb, seven thousand notebook pages exist, and most scholars judge this to be only half the number produced.

The handwritten letters, records, and architectural drawings of Thomas Jefferson likewise lure me, including his Monticello garden and farm journals. I admire Jefferson's distinct adoration and respect for Italy, evident in many of the approximate nineteen thousand letters he penned. And who else has christened their home "Monticello"? (It was the famous Virginian's Italian interpretation for "hillock" or "little mountain.") Who else has so exuberantly declared Andrea Palladio's *Four Books of Architecture* to be his architectural "bible"?

Included among Jefferson's surviving personal effects is a small leather-bound journal and a tiny reusable "notepad" made of ivory. I especially find the latter enticing—how the pocket-size case holds thin pieces of ivory together in fan-like fashion, similar to pages in a tablet. The smooth ivory "pages" can be written on and later erased. How easily I picture Jefferson on horseback, checking the condition of his crops, pausing to pencil notes in his portable pad—observations later transferred to paper.

Scrapbooks. At a recent BookExpo America exhibit, sponsored by the American Booksellers Association, I discovered entire catalogs and booths dedicated to the craft of "scrapbooking." Since my idea of a scrapbook is a *box*, or a three-ring binder with clear pocket pages, the conformity of the pre-packaged materials disturbed me. It was all too serious and generic. "Who," I asked myself, "are these people having the time on their hands to snip, paste, and organize with thematic stickers and framed pages?"

Obviously not me. Never one to save "pieces" of Italy in typical scrapbook manner, I've adopted a bare-bones habit instead. I clip newspapers and create stacks. I tear pages from magazines and make piles. It's only when the trip hazard of my stacks and piles causes me to land face flat on the floor that I tackle the daunting task of reducing my "termite mounds," before they invade the whole house. My poor husband holds the fairy tale expectation that my Italy infestation should be limited to dedicated office space. (Surely he jests!)

Finally, when I can no longer stand the mounds myself, I plunge forward with sorting and organizing. I fill file folders and binder pages with news clippings of Italy: city and regional information, and references to architecture, gardening, fashion, soccer, weather, and politics. I also tear out articles and photographs from travel and home magazines—gathering ideas for future journeys, and for creating my own Italian *cucina* and *bagno*.

The best odd-sized stuff lands in boxes, containers I call "scrapboxes." "Make it easy," I say. Keep it simple to collect the tidbits of Italy: brochures, playbills, opera programs, product labels, recipes, and restaurant menus. Store Italy-related goods loose in a box so that you can pick them up, turn them over, and dream. With a scrapbox on your lap, you lift the lid and find magic—delicious and delirious travel without leaving home.

You don't have to be a poet to write a poem! Try it. Fill notebook pages with a slice of your soul through poetry. Your work may not be of laureate status, but lyric verse lies within us whether we realize it or not. The poetic form is about dreaming, caring, loving, revealing inner thoughts and emotions—either happy or sad, colorful or dim. Each one of us has something to share, words that express inner feelings. Whether the words tumble out in honest emotion, free without reserve, or whether we must extract each one like a rotten tooth, the end result can be poetry.

Begin with a list poem. Grab a notebook and start a personal melody of descriptive phrases—your intimate dreams of Italy.

"But what," you ask, "is a list poem?"

It's easy. Think of a subject and make a roster of favorite images, emotions, or activities that remind you of Italy. Do this in the form of a grocery list and you'll be composing a list poem. Simple. No rhyme, rhythm, or meter required. Include word groupings that focus on specific scenery or actions, something you fantasize about. A hilltop Tuscan villa with an olive grove and private vineyard? A quiet pasta dinner by candlelight under a faded Umbrian sky?

If you have trouble creating phrases that describe your subject, start with simple words. Susan Wooldridge, in her book *Poemcrazy: Freeing Your Life with Words*, describes how she collects words. She "borrows" and creates her words, assembling them into something she calls a "wordpool."

You can do the same by exploring your senses. Look, smell, touch, listen, and taste. Collect active and descriptive words that remind you of a place where you've been in Italy or may have experienced through a book. Glean favorite words or phrases while watching a movie or reading—words that leap off the page or screen. Then add new words as you find them. Make a long list so you can later edit it by eliminating and rearranging.

List words that suggest color in subtle or different ways. Write mushroom, not brown; try pumpkin for orange; use sunflower or lemon instead of yellow. Collect words that *sound* good—singing words, buzzing words, words that are fun to whisper or roll on your tongue. Pick and choose and combine your words into phrases. Pick and choose and combine your phrases into poetry.

As a grade school teacher, my mother collected what is typically known as "story starters." She wrote word phrases and sentences on colored index cards and dropped them in a basket for her students to use as prompts. Italy lovers start stories all the time but fail to write them down.

List poetry is one way to start a story that can later be read, told, lived, or dreamed. When is the last time you dreamed a story of your making? Don't wait for a dream to happen—start one instead.

It's revealing to write a list poem before traveling to Italy, then again upon returning, while images are vivid and undiminished by time. The poems that follow are in such a sequence. As expected, the one I wrote immediately after a trip is less abstract. Both poems are ordinary, but meaningful to me in the same way that yours will be meaningful to you.

The poems I share demonstrate one example of form; many others exist. Most notably, Walt Whitman used sentences to create positive imagery in *Leaves of Grass*. The book of Genesis in the Bible, in contrast, lists tribes, names, and life spans to create poetry in list form. Remember that list poetry is not exclusive. You can list anything. Instead of, or in addition to, physical descriptions—people, objects, or scenery—you may choose to focus on emotions or activities.

Written during a flight to Milan, following a long absence from Italy:

MEMORIES OF ITALY

Rolling farmland and grapevine rows
Fenceless fields of lemon-colored blossoms
Cypress trees and olive groves
A sea of Siena rooftops
Stone streets and winding stairways
People talking with their hands and smoking cigarettes
Olive oil and pastas and open-air markets
Limonati and *limone* gelati
Gentle music for dining and strolling
Awkward glances at strangers
Music drifting from doorways
Stucco walls and *palazzi* dreamhouses

Country dining and singing *fratelli*
Checked tablecloths and bottles of table wine
Mystery, intrigue, and whispers
Reflected sunlight and shadows along canals
Fluttering pigeons in Piazza San Marco
Secret and puzzling pathways
Stone water fountains and tiptoeing alley cats
Gondolas and striped-shirted *gondoliere*
Echoes of lapping water

Written following the same trip, with images of
Tuscany and the Veneto still fresh on my mind:

MORE MEMORIES OF ITALY

Reflected sunlight and twenty yellow colors in a stucco wall
Women strolling arm in arm in purposeful conversation
Bicycle riders pedaling and crisscrossing the *piazza*
Children hugging basilica columns
Smells of *prosciutto* and *Asiago* cheese from fringed doorways
Clinking dishes behind openings flanked by shutters
Chatter from bars where people stand drinking espresso
Afternoon naps in the cool of shutter-darkened bedrooms
Clothes hanging out of windows like flags in a fashion parade
Thin crusty pizza to eat with fork and knife
Local vegetables of every color and shape
Summer fruits that linger into fall
Giant grapes so sweet they startle the senses
Apricot and custard pastries from a *pasticceria*
Bottles of local olive oil and crusty breads in a basket

Pasta shapes that swirl, twist, and fold
The aroma of *olio d'oliva*, garlic, and tomatoes in a pizzeria
Smells drifting from a *trattoria* or *paninoteca*
The flavor and spongy texture of fresh *Mozzarella di bufala*
Figs, blood oranges, and pomegranate seeds
Towering chestnut trees dropping golden brown nuggets
Planted trees giving symmetrical structure to a rolling landscape
Architectural and agrarian landscapes in harmony
Terrazzo floors collaged with color and texture
Gentle frescoes on ceiling coffers
Evening *passeggiata* and gelato escapes

Travel Through Books

One of my favorite pastimes is adopting the role of a bookstalker. I haunt new and used bookstores at home and while traveling—anything about Italy. Like a predator I pace with an alphabetized list, searching the aisles for known authors. Then at random I cruise for potential dust jackets, shelf after shelf and book by book. It's tedious, time-consuming, and I love it.

But what happens next is beyond my control. When I hit upon books about Italy, or ones written by Italian writers, they leap into my arms and cling to me like Velcro. Like Venus flytraps ready to snare victims, my hands lunge forward and grab. In any case, I'm doomed, with over 500 bound captives so far.

For better or worse, books seize David too. They're the lowest common denominator in our lives—a basic bond and the factor dividing the people we know into two distinct groups, readers and nonreaders. It's a distinction that outlasts the differences between people *with* and *without* children, because books, unlike offspring, are lifetime companions that never leave home. They sneak into your house, one or two (or an armful of Italy titles) at a time, and never go away.

Asking my husband (or any book lover) to cull a few "old books" for a neighborhood garage sale is like asking him to give up his high school tee-shirt collection or his burnt-orange polyester leisure suit from 1976. It's not about to happen any time soon!

When we decided to move to our current location, I crawled under the house right away, in the company of a structural engineer, to check the load capacity of each pier and beam. I was nervous that the his-and-hers book collection we'd acquired would sink our live-in ship. The thought of our vertical brick dwelling becoming a Leaning Tower of Pisa was unsettling to say the least. And when calculations confirmed my fear, there was but one obvious solution: pour yet another bundle of dough into our money pit of accumulated books. Since purging was not an option we could face, we added additional piers, strategically located concrete supports, to be able to occupy the two-story "library" we call home.

Big books. Like a sunflower pulled by the sun, my husband is drawn to oversized volumes of photographic collections and gargantuan tomes depicting distant geographies— China, Russia, or Mongolia. And for birthday and Christmas presents for me, David buys the huge, lap-sharing Italy volumes I adore—books large enough for two people to enjoy side by side (which we frequently do!). All in all, the pine chest in front of our living room sofa holds a lifetime of journey, lumbering pulp pyramids of foreign-photo chronicles waiting to be opened and explored.

Excluding bicycle excursions, however, David's idea of pilgrimage *is* a coffee-table book. His fondness for big travel books is fickle, existing to the extent that he doesn't have to pack a bag. I'm convinced he'd go lots of places if he could simply snap his fingers and land somewhere terrific on his bicycle—and if, just as instantly, he could snap for his clothes the same way.

Since neither one of us grew up taking notable vacations involving great distance or time, I'm not sure how it happened—how polar differences evolved. How I developed a yearning for peregrinations (a gypsy compared to David!), while my partner did not, is perplexing. But I blame architecture most of all.

Once I started studying the history and conservation practices of architecture, a passion emerged that quickly zoomed out of control. Old buildings and other cultural artifacts consumed me like dope. (Would I ever be normal again!) Finally, as a grad-school junkie with double degrees focused on historic preservation, my husband said, "Enough! We can no longer afford your habit."

I also blame books for my wanderlust. First hooked on architectural history and decorative arts books while in college and graduate school, I eventually started mainlining travel literature: William Dean Howells, Henry James, D. H. Lawrence, Edith Wharton, Mary McCarthy. Then I discovered Peter Mayle's hilarious experiences with renovating a house in France (*A Year in Provence*). Reading Mayle's well-quipped prose, a few years after its initial publication, caused me to rethink life goals. (Was it time for another trip to Italy?) About the same time, I read a magazine article about a woman who used her credit card to spot-purchase a dilapidated stone hovel in France (though I like to think it was in Italy)—her writer's retreat. Hmm, I said out loud, with a rumble of *carpe diem* in my head, toying with a range of possibilities. I love books. I love writing. I love Italy.

Then, like a thunderstorm rattling my existence, my windows on life, Frances Mayes entered my life. In 1996 I bought a first-edition copy of *Under the Tuscan Sun: At Home in Italy* and started reading it before I'd even left the bookstore's parking lot. Finally, still cradling the crisp pages in my lap, I drove home to gulp every word in a marathon word sprint. *Under the Tuscan Sun* wraps sensuous memoir, dream journal, and spirit-catcher, all, within its cover. And considering the masses of tourists landing in Italy today, I'm not the only Italophile who recognized a personal passion by reading and rereading Mayes' story—her *magnum opus.*

More recently, like reading butterfly messages from Italy, I lost myself to her equally poetic *Bella Tuscany.* Following Mayes' words as they dipped and fluttered, I tasted Italian nectar for myself. Dare I hope that there's more?

I never leave home without something to read—books or magazines about, or related to, Italy. Pockets, purses, briefcases, luggage, and cars were designed for this very purpose! Cars, especially, are well suited to the task, for they hold more.

Each week I toss a few books in the back seat of my old gray Land Cruiser, and by mid-month my books-on-wheels buddy assumes the identity of an old-fashioned bookmobile. Like stocking a pantry for unexpected appetites, I also fill my car with audio provisions—an ample supply of cassette tapes that are perfect for learn-to-speak-Italian instruction, Italian music or opera, and books on tape. Have you *listened* to a book lately—about Italy?

"Talking" books are my lifeline in desperate situations, when book-separation anxiety sets in and hands are otherwise engaged. While audio books are not my typical means of literary consumption, I take what I can get on the road. Besides, it is fun with favorite authors to first read and then later listen to their words on tape. The staff at bookstores love it when I buy the same book twice, one in each format.

Bella Tuscany is a prime example of why audio books should never be dismissed. Reading Frances Mayes' second Italy installment was pure reading pleasure, but later *listening* to the same unabridged words on cassette tape was a completely different journey, a separate adventure. Was the *Bella Tuscany* audio experience also heightened, perhaps, because I'd recently met her at a book signing? Was it because I'd finally heard Mayes' *live* voice, not the recorded inflections I'd previously given ear to with *Under the Tuscan Sun*?

On the go, I catch Italy-reading and -listening moments wherever I am. I read sitting, standing, walking—while waiting for a doctor's appointment (I never rely on their magazine selection), while queuing at the post office (others read over my shoulder to see what's so good that I can't put it down), while idling in line at a drive-in bank (drivers behind me are polite to honk when it's time to move forward), while being on hold on the phone (easily worth a few chapters a day), while attending to an oil change at a service station, while toasting under foil flaps and a hooded hair dryer to acquire a new and improved hair color. If it weren't for all the "free" waiting times in my daily life, I'd never get to read much at all. I'd never know anything about Italy!

I like details not found in typical publications, particulars not intended for *turismo*. I want to read about and travel to places where sightseers seldom wander, locations best discovered by accident. Instead of hitting the obvious attractions as soon as I step off the train, I'd rather aim for a distant cathedral spire that entices with subtle simplicity. I'd rather saunter back alleys and out-of-the-way *piazze* in search of local markets. While planning a trip to Italy is half the joy of journey, I also want to stumble once I get there. Stumbling into a good experience is never a letdown! Instantaneous discoveries become the memory-makers that keep Italy dreamers dreaming.

A good destination-oriented essay, novel, or mystery often tells me more about a city or region than most travel guidebooks. Guidebooks alone are too little. Sometimes they even mislead, when passages are read out of context—or by the wrong spouse!

On the next-to-last night of our anniversary trip, the night before heading back to Milan, David asked if he could look at one of the ragged books I'd toted in my pack for nearly two weeks. Not only was it David's first time to ask about the city, it was his first inquiry about any of our plans. In the many months since January, when he first agreed to go to Italy, I never fielded one question from his lips. He waited, instead, until we were on our way home.

"Can I read about the hotel you picked in Milan?" asked David.

"What for?" I replied, raising an eyebrow. "You want to stay a little longer?" I joked in hopes he wasn't *really* interested in reading about our reserved place of lodging.

"No, I just want to see where we're booked for our last night. You said the hotel is close to the train station, but how close? It doesn't sound very safe to me."

I poured the next words slowly—like a dribble of honey. "Haven't you liked all the places so far? What makes you think I'd pick a bad hotel now?"

"Yes, but I *still* want to read about the one in Milan." David stubbornly persisted.

Fumbling for the guidebook in question, my mind scrambled for potential excuses, to offset the confrontation that was sure to come when David read about the neighborhood I'd chosen. Could I sway him with the merits of convenience? Should I emphasize that the proprietor speaks English?

Finally, I relinquished the lethal pages, the bomb that might explode. Then I held my breath.

"Didn't you read this at all?" he said, seconds later.

"Did you see this about the area being seedy and frumpy? And frequented by aging hookers?" He was furious. "What were you thinking when you picked this hotel? You know I like to stay in clean places. This doesn't even sound safe. So what makes you think it'll be clean?" Calmly, I assured him that the travel manual wouldn't list establishments that were dangerous. And finally he agreed, conceding mostly because it was too late to change the reservation.

After savoring an incredible dinner at one of the local restaurants in our "seedy" neighborhood—one of the finest meals during our entire vacation—we headed back the few short blocks to our hotel.

"See, this neighborhood's not so bad," I bragged. "We only saw that one woman outside our hotel when we arrived this afternoon, and she looked perfectly harmless."

"Yes, yes, you're right. Just like all our other reservations, this one's been fine. I like it a lot and they're friendly and speak English. It's been great."

Then, as we rounded the final corner to see our hotel in full view, there they were. I'd bragged too soon. Three over-fifty ladies of the evening were draped on the next-door stoop and sidewalk like gaudy window curtains from the sixties. Momentarily halted by laughter and tears, we eventually slithered toward and past them in bound silence to our own stepped landing—exploding once again in the privacy of our room.

More than movies, or any other means of pre-travel consumption, it's the books I read that endear me to Italian experiences. Another person's adventure becomes my own. Whether historical or contemporary, fact or fiction, I prefer writing that concentrates on a specific location with a narrow personal focus. The tighter the focus, the better.

"So where," you ask, "is a recommended reading list for armchair travel to Italy?"

For three glaring reasons (or excuses), it's impossible for me to create a "best" reading list—a universal guide. First, the shear number of in-print, out-of-print, and forthcoming books about Italy is overwhelming. I didn't realize the potential magnitude of my collecting mania until I was in over my head! Books on the subject have poured from a bottomless pitcher for centuries, with no end to the flow in sight. I can't possibly live long enough to read all the ones that already exist, much less all the books to come.

But I know I'll die trying. I'll go for the gold. I suspect that when I'm ninety-five years old I'll barely be able to maneuver our house, not because I expect to be feeble, but because I forecast a treacherous maze of stacked books, magazines, and newspapers covering every inch of our floors—towering word trees in a literary jungle. Out of control.

The second argument for why I can't produce a best reading list is that for obvious and countless other reasons, my reading experience will be different than yours. What I like, you may hate. Books that race my heart may leave you cold. My reading is prejudiced by the sum of *my* years, not yours.

Thirdly, I will change my mind tomorrow, or next year about the contents of the list, as my steadfast gobbling of words fattens me with altered perspectives.

But now that I've said all this, I *will* share what I can. While I can't tell you, universally, what is best to read about Italy, I'll randomly offer some of what I know, some of what I feel from my gut. For whatever the reason that I was charmed while reading, I'll convey a few titles, enjoyed in whole or part—volumes that feed my Italy fever. (See Books That Depict Italy.)

In the same way that a plate of *antipasti* makes me crave additional courses, a 1997 trio of anthologies whets my appetite for more writing about Italy. *Italy in Mind*, edited by Alice Leccese Powers, offers a savory sampling of short stories, novels, essays, journals, letters, and poetry—a seductive read, one and all.

A second collection, *Desiring Italy*, highlights twenty-eight female writers of distinction. Edited by Susan Cahill and destined to become a classic endorsement, the anthology is smartly organized geographically. Each literary passage is also followed by a slew of helpful endnotes—travel and historical tidbits, suggested literary paths to follow.

And *Beyond the Godfather: Italian American Writers on the Real Italian American Experience*, edited by A. Kenneth Ciongoli and Jay Parini, covers a medley of topics by contemporary writers: personal, literary, and political essays. Perhaps more pungent and less romantic than the previous two anthologies, this collection's best attribute for me is that it includes a number of Italian American writers I'd never read before.

My first real foothold on the world of Italian women writers, however, was by way of an earlier source. Compiled by multiple editors and indexed by region and country, *500 Great Books by Women: A Reader's Guide*, is where I first discovered the works of Italian authors: Natalia Ginzburg, Grazia Deledda, Anna Banti, Rosetta Loy, and Anna Maria Ortese. The guide also exposed me to Ann Cornelisen. Additional listings—Barbara Grizzuti Harrison's *Italian Days*, Anne Rice's *Cry to Heaven*, and Elizabeth Von Arnim's *Enchanted April*—were already familiar favorites.

The first time I read one of Natalia Ginzburg's books, I was drawn to her simple prose. Her collection of essays, *The Little Virtues*, is a good beginning for new Ginzburg readers. Ranging from an essay written in Rome during the autumn of 1944, to the title essay written in London in the spring of 1960, the topics reveal Ginzburg's captivating style. One of my favorite essays, "He and I," evokes an amalgam of emotions. It is simultaneously humorous, sad, and endearing. The essay begins with a situation that is familiar in my own house: one spouse is hot and the other is cold. Ginzburg's husband is my husband, for the moment, each time I raise the igloo temperature that my spouse keeps setting on the thermostat.

Besides dictionaries, I have a hodgepodge of works that compare English and Italian text side by side. It's a clever concept without a doubt, even if it's lost on me. (Will I ever be able to decipher Italian!) The *Penguin Parallel Text: Italian Short Stories I* and *Italian Short Stories II* have been reprinted a number of times. One piece by Natalia Ginzburg, "The Mother," is included in the first collection, and both volumes are good preludes to Italian authors. The language in the second collection is expanded, less literal than in the first, and introduces more writers.

Out of the millions of words that have been written about Italy, I gravitate to anything travel- and Italy-related by Henry James, D. H. Lawrence, and Edith Wharton. And my vintage copies of W. D. Howells' *Italian Journeys*, Caroline Atwater Mason's *The Spell of Italy*, and Katherine Hooker's *Byways in Southern Tuscany* are especially dear to me. Don't even think about asking to borrow them!

My most secret and treasured Italy-depicting book is likewise rare. Frances Elliot's double volume, *Diary of an*

Idle Woman in Italy, is a lustrous pearl on my shelf, a gem discovered in the deep ocean of used bookstores where I've dived. As introduction, Elliot shares words that match my own disposition, or at least one longing that is nothing short of a dream. How precious it would be to go to Italy baggage-free—without mental (or physical) encumbrances. No worry about bills to be paid at home. No frets about business matters unattended. No guilt about leaving loved ones behind!

When I call these volumes "The Diary of an Idle Woman," I do so because I went to Italy with a perfectly disengaged mind, with no special objects of inquiry, no definite call or profession, no pre-conceived theories. I was idle in that I went where fancy or accident led me; otherwise I hope my readers will not consider me "an idle woman."

FRANCES ELLIOT
from *The Diary of an Idle Woman in Italy*

And for depictions of cities? Topping my scroll among Italian city portraits is Mary McCarthy's *Venice Observed*. In tandem is McCarthy's fine tribute, *The Stones of Florence*. No one else says so much with so few words: each book is a crash course in culture and philosophy for a particular destination.

A tattered and crinkled paperback I searched for and bought via the Internet is another ripe plum in my garden of Italian delights. Page by page, Kate Simon's *Italy: The Places in Between* is fruitful reward. Her essays are potent and spicy, sprinkled with marvelous insight.

Because I love architecture, I also treasure a small publication from Great Britain that is more sketchbook than journal: *An Architect in Italy* by Caroline Mauduit. Recorded on the pages of this watercolor-filled chronicle are parts of Mauduit's architectural tour of Italy during 1983 and 1984. The sketchbook's release in 1988 coincided with my own architectural initiation in Italy.

My desire to read stories with Italian settings also inspired me to explore mysteries once again, a genre I'd dismissed for years. I grew up with Nancy Drew and the Hardy Boys, so I'm not sure how I strayed so far from the sleuthful adventures I relished as a child. In part, I blame television. I started watching detective shows instead of reading detective stories. Mike Connors first lured me in *Mannix* during high school and college, and then came Peter Falk in *Columbo*.

Eventually, I developed a fixation for Tom Selleck in *Magnum, PI*. The image of Thomas Sullivan Magnum driving a Ferrari 308 is my pinup poster-of-choice for a secret closet, if I had one. Instead, the closest thing I have is a snack tray—a Tom Selleck snack tray, a gag gift from a dear crony of mine. Sadly, however, my tiny folding table doesn't picture a Ferrari—just a smiling, mustached, and curly-headed face with twinkling eyes. Only recently did I purchase a befitting Italian sports car to accompany my esteemed collectable.

But instead of offering *lire* in Maranello (south of Modena), site of the famous Ferrari plant, I cut a deal in the glamourous-sounding city of Ferrara. Now parked on my Selleck snack tray is a shiny red convertible marked "MADE IN ITALY"—the only car I ever brought home in a backpack!

While digging through clues for mystery novels with Italian settings, at some point I unearthed a reading guide by Willetta L. Heising that provides mystery-series listings by type, characters, occupations, and settings. A bonanza!

Through Heising's *Detecting Women 2: A Reader's Guide and Checklist for Mystery Series Written by Women*, writer Donna Leon first apprehended me with *Death at La Fenice*, one book in a series portraying Italian police commissioner Guido Brunetti. For my anniversary trip with David, I was determined to see the charred remains of Venice's famous opera house, La Fenice (The Phoenix), and *Death at La Fenice* set the mood for me. It was perfect for in-flight reading—small to pack, a quick no-fuss read.

A compatible source, Sisters in Crime, is a worldwide organization that promotes female mystery writers.

Through their Web site and "Mystery Website Links," it's possible to spend hours investigating mystery-related activities. The organization produces a catalog of current and forthcoming books by their membership.

The moment I spied *Dead Lagoon*, a murder mystery by Michael Dibdin, I knew its setting was also Venice. Only one lagoon, in my eyes, could warrant the name. Italian police detective Aurelio Zen also heads numerous other adventures for Dibdin in Italian locations. (I mentioned another title, *A Long Finish*, in chapter five—with reference to Alba, truffles, and wine.)

Another book, *Vaporetto 13* by Robert Girardi, jumped off a bookstore shelf into my arms. It *screamed* of Venice and is written in the tradition of a ghost story. Need I say more?

The city of canals is further mystified by Edward Sklepowich. *A Black Bridge: A Mystery of Venice* is Sklepowich's fourth volume in his Urbino Macintyre series. Sklepowich knows Venice inside out. I first followed the footsteps of Macintyre in the "mummy" cabal titled *Death in a Serene City*.

And then there's Valerie Martin's coaxing novel *Italian Fever*. (How could I resist her title!) Besides being a sucker for female sleuths, I fancy who-done-its featuring Americans abroad. Martin's heroine, Lucy, extracts pleasure from Italy through a love of art and a tango with romance.

News from the Vatican intrigues me. Like a bat zapping insects at night, I scan the *The New York Times* with radar eyes, searching for photographic morsels of the latest bishops to lie prostrate before the Pope at St. Peter's Basilica. Maybe it's my upbringing. Southern Protestant exposure is dour antithesis to the Roman Catholic Church, with its elaborate ceremonies and grand architectural expressions—*chiesa* and basilica structures famously known throughout the world.

After reading Brian Murphy's book *The New Men: Inside the Vatican's Elite School for American Priests*, I proceeded to conquer *Day of Confession* by Allan Folsom, not by reading it but by listening to the unabridged version read by actor Joe Mantegna. Six months later, the spectacle of a Vatican under siege remains torched on my brain like a bonfire—a fiery furnace that refuses to die. I never thought a crime thriller would clutch me in suspense, but it did. And Mantegna's diction style cinched it.

The posthumous release of William D. Maltalbano's ecclesiastical thriller, *Basilica*, is another deep well to fall into. Especially if, like me, you're wrenched by the constraints and perplexities of the Vatican dynasty, and overwhelmed by its authority. As a tiny sovereign state within Italy, created in 1929 and covering less than one hundred and ten acres of land, Vatican City holds a powerful presence that is difficult for "outsiders" to comprehend. The Pope's stronghold maintains its own police authority, post office, and radio station; mints unique Italian coins and prints special Vatican news publications. It even has its own flag (a white and yellow one), and a blanket speed limit of 20-miles-per-hour for motorists.

New memoirs and novels in bountiful supply keep popping up to tempt me, and I shall plead that they never end. So I offer a few more fresh selections, ripe berries to plop in the mouth. Ferenc Máté outdid himself in telling his real-life adventure *The Hills of Tuscany: A New Life in an Old Land.* He and his painter wife, Candace, are presented in delightful and often humorous prose for all Italy lovers to savor.

Martha T. Cummings' novel *Straddling the Borders: The Year I Grew Up in Italy* is a spirit-soaring story that fondles real life. Her personal insight into tracing ancestral roots yields both heartwarming and amusing moments. I wanted to pack a bag and go with her.

The Palace, Lisa St. Aubin de Terán's enchanting novel set in the time of Garibaldi, evokes a very different image of Italy. Cloaked with nineteenth-century details, it's the fable of a peasant soldier's struggle to build a dream palace for the woman he loves.

Then there's a scant handful of previous literary buddies I haven't squeezed in. They keep waving to me from their alphabetized positions on my bookshelves, making it almost obligatory that I somehow answer their calling in my rambling epistle! So forgive me: here they are, in abbreviated form.

Gay Talese's strongest self-revealing work, *Unto the Sons*, is impossible to shun. Naturally, I'm drawn to his Italian American heritage. The saga of his father's life poignantly depicts the southern Italian immigrant experience, and exposes the reader to the folio of heart-wrenching decisions that so many newcomers had to face when leaving loved ones behind in order to come to America. So aptly Talese paints the struggle between allegiance to old and new homeland.

I'm also fascinated by writer Wallis Wilde-Menozzi, an American woman who married into a Parma family in the 1980s. She offers an insider's perspective in her non-fluffy account called *Mother Tongue: An American Life in Italy*. Wilde-Menozzi reveals bare cords of exile and acceptance issues—am I American? Am I Italian? Is it *possible* to be both? On the lighter side, her writing is suggestive of Tim Parks, the English writer who married into a Veronese family. Parks' real-life family stories are personified in *An Italian Education* and his earlier *Italian Neighbors*.

Italians Umberto Eco and Primo Levi demand attention, together with Italo Calvino. (I've mentioned Calvino in a previous chapter.) While I've never been able to conquer Eco's lengthy monsters, I did enjoy his pocket-size collection *How to Travel with a Salmon and Other Essays*. His reflections on the ordinary happenings of daily life amused me: "How to Eat Ice Cream, How to Spend Time, How to Recognize a Porn Movie." The latter essay especially rebounded when I recently read how the Roman Catholic Church reviews all Italian movies for content. I pictured this Bishop seated in the middle of a theater, alone in a skirt of darkness, waiting for the unmentionable to be mentioned, waiting for the unthinkable to leap forward on screen.

When I first read Primo Levi, I was similarly seduced by a particular essay collection, one called *Other People's Trades*, where the Turin-born writer discusses everything from skulls and writing to fleas and chemistry. (Levi was trained as a chemist.) As was true for me with Eco, I initially enjoyed Levi's short compositions, and only now am I trying to devour his "meatier" volumes, *The Periodic Table* and *The Monkey's Wrench*.

Post-Bramasole—forever nipped by Frances Mayes—I continue to suck up all the Italy books I can flush from under cover. I keep stalking used bookstores for out-of-print booty. I scour magazines and newspapers for reviews and place orders for books not yet printed. Then at last, when

CHAPTER EIGHT

Indulge in Milanese Fashion (or Plant a Garden)

G ucci, Prado, Armani, Dolce & Gabbana, Versace...
the list goes on. From shoes and clothing to eye-
wear and accessories, it's all about famous names.
Looking at myself in the mirror today, I realize I'm in trouble. What was I thinking when I decided to write about fashion? Where are *my* designer labels?

So far, my only *real* experience with Italian "style" was
a haircut one time in Pisa. Yes, Pisa. I saw the Leaning
Tower and bought a couple of postcards, sat for a jazzy
hair snipping, and stuffed toilet paper in the oversized key-
hole of my hotel door that night. The visit was quick, but
the haircut was memorable.

Cloaked with a cape like a swashbuckling Zorro, I sat

armed with two critical words: *corto* and *lungo*, short and long; I barely knew that *capelli* meant hair. The stylist, on the other hand, spoke a thimbleful of English. "How lucky for me," I whispered, before realizing his acquisitions had nothing to do with cosmetology.

In the beginning, the scenario went like this. The hairdresser would ask a question in Italian. And I'd answer in English. He'd pose another question (or maybe it was a repeat), and I'd answer again the same way—as if I were deaf and didn't hear the first time. Then, hoping role reversal would solve our dilemma, I stabbed at a few comments of my own, squirting my best Texas lingo. While it *sounded* like conversation, as if what we were doing made sense, neither of us had a clue what the other was saying.

But then seconds later, out of nowhere, the event took off like a mime show. We started "talking" with our hands and nodding our heads. And *capelli* started dropping to the floor.

If you ask how we communicated, I can't tell you. If you think I got butchered, you'd be wrong. In spite of the potential for disaster, my flirtation with fashion—my fling with an Italian barber—resulted in a stylish trim job!

While *all* window shopping in Italy exceeds *any* kind of shopping at home, the posted prices in *lire* evidently deter me. Or do they? My first reaction is to say things cost too much, yet secretly I fear it's an excuse. If pockets full of *lire* were the only issue, why hadn't I visited designer outlet stores near Milan and Florence? (Yes, they exist!)

Was it the money or something else?

Searching for clues, I march to my closet for a definitive review of the circumstantial evidence, a cold objective look—at my clothes. And the obvious before me is frightening. My closet is the scene of a crime.

Like a bald tire on a slippery road, my winter coat (*sans* label) is worn slick; instead of a sleek, fuzzy nap, I have fuzzballs. Looking at the closet floor is no better. There are no Amalfi *scarpe*, no Ferragamos waiting to be walked in—not one pair of daring stiletto heels, not even a pair of mild-mannered leather pumps. All the evidence shouts "earth woman" shoes, loud and clear—round-toed walkers without any hint of a heel.

For the very first time I realize that all my clothes— hanging on racks, lying in drawers, drooping from hooks, waiting in a hamper to be washed—all of them look the same. Every garment is simple and limp, loosely constructed without form. They all mush together like mashed potatoes with no hint of butter or chives—no accent color, no suggestion of foreign flavor. In spite of my obsession with all else Italian, my wardrobe is domestic and boring. I'm guilty. The proof is overwhelming, impossible to ignore.

Expecting the fashion police to arrive at any moment, I confess under oath: "I was born with a defective glamour gene. I admit it—I hate going shopping for clothes." Too willingly, perhaps, I buy books, kitchen gadgets, and hardware items, but not stylish accouterments for the body.

"Did you know my wardrobe is the pits?" I demanded of David, the night of my closet revelation.

But he only grinned and replied with his usual response, "Okay, so what else is new?"

Struggling over my fashionless fate, I pondered the situation. When I was in Italy, why did I drool at the touch of handsome fabrics and spend endless hours in a fabric shop? With each trip, why did I purr over the sensuousness of Italian leather goods and think I'd buy a handbag, but then change my mind? Why did I stare at myself in dozens of new sunglasses—Luxottica frames of endless color and configuration—but in the end return to Texas with the same old pair I'd worn for years?

Finally, I made sense of it all to my satisfaction. More than the finished product, I've decided that it's the architectural integrity of Italian *materials* that entice me—a finely woven textile, a softly tanned leather, an exquisite silver buckle on a belt. It's an attraction to the materials and craftsmanship in Italy that best explains my ability to spend hours window shopping in Siena or Vicenza, and only minutes with a mail-order catalog at home.

Without warning, a seasonal fever nibbles at me today as I read in *The New York Times* that capris, pedal pushers, and toreadors are the rage for spring. I may have a lackluster fashion gene, but my spirit soars at the mere thought of wearing short pants.

I'm reminded of old Girl Scout camp days in fourth grade, my earliest years of wearing cropped trousers. For my first departure to Camp Kachina, outfitted in camp "uniform" in front of Mother's Kodak Brownie, I posed for a first-time-away-from-home snapshot wearing mismatched cotton prints: an untucked buttoned shirt and elastic-waist pedal pushers (clamdiggers sounded funny in Central Texas) that were just the right length—not too short, not too long.

Re-reading the news article, I dream that the pedal pushers I'll wear this spring will be *ultima moda*, straight off the runway in Milan—side-vented khakis, olive gabardines or twills. A sophisticated Gidget or Audrey Hepburn appearance.

But in truth I know better. Instead of a shopping spree at a nearby mall, I'll simply make do. I'll snip off the bottom of an old pair of pants, stitch a hem, and pretend. And I won't call them pedal pushers, as I did when I was ten. This time around, homemade or not, I'll be sporting new "Italian" capris!

When thoughts of a new wardrobe make me dizzy, I whisper to myself, "Plant a garden." I slip into an old pair of Birkenstock sandals and head to a favorite nursery in search of seeds from Italy.

When I was growing up, everybody I knew had a garden—my parents and grandparents, aunts and uncles, the neighbors down the road, teachers, and friends' families. Now, decades later, I realize how that strong tradition of growing one's own food left deep marks on my young southern soul. Tilling soil and planting seeds is a part of me.

When I was ten or eleven, a girlfriend of mine wore a tiny mustard seed around her neck—a tiny water-filled half-bubble on a silver mount, hanging from a silver chain. Inside, a seed floated. To me the seed pendant was more than jewelry. It was a simple expression of life: if the tiny particle was planted, it would grow. It held another meaning too. For the first time in my life, "mustard" was something other than the yellow stuff we spread on hamburgers. It was a *color*. The mustard embryo itself was not orange or yellow—it was *mustard*, a dirty blend between the two.

My Italy is like that mustard seed. In the way that the seed was not simply orange or yellow, the colors of the Italy I know are layered and blended by nature. And gardening? Gardening is the celebration of nature that takes me to the layered earthy hues, to the mustard colors of Italy.

Several years ago, still mindful of the fortieth birthday I'd celebrated not *that* long before, I expanded my tiny garden patch in the city. The "big forty" milestone makes you do crazy things. I mean, who has *time* to plant a garden? Who has the time to water and to pluck weeds?

But the answer is easy. Any woman over forty must *find* the time. Post-forty, my dirty dishes started growing in the sink as if they'd been fertilized. Business and dress attire developed allergic reactions to spray starch. And newspapers suddenly piled up to become fire hazards. If gardening is something you love, then you whittle, steal, or *conjure* the time to do it, whatever it takes, even if you must start with a couple of terra cotta pots on a patio or deck. That's what I did.

The quality of imported terra cotta is worth the price. The cheap pots I purchased pre-Italy-fever have all cracked, but the Italian urns bought long ago are aging with grace. A round or square container with a classical rope or garland decoration makes a perfect *orto*, or kitchen garden, or a *giardino minuscolo*, a small flower garden.

My garden "expansions" are usually simple each year, but this time was different. In lieu of another clay pot or garden ornament, or yet another new lavender to test (interpret kill!), I doubled my tilled square footage. I carved a bold border garden on the front edge of our yard and along the driveway, the sunniest spot I could find. Old dirt was taken out and worm-worthy soil brought in.

Alongside herbs and perennials, I sowed seeds from Italy—vegetable seeds imported by a local nursery. *Fagioli*, a Romano Bush Bean variety; *lattuga*, a butter-flavored lettuce; *rucola*, a tangy or peppery salad green sometimes called rocket salad; and a little round *zucchino* variety labeled *Tondo Chiaro di Nizza*.

As it did Christopher Columbus, and later Thomas Jefferson, the cross-cultural idea of seeds and plants from other countries suits me. It seems odd, however, to think of zucchini being brought *back* to the New World— boomerang seeds flying through the air in cultural exchange. If only Columbus could see how "Italianized" his squash (and other) transplants had become! How fascinating it would be for Thomas Jefferson to see Monticello's Web site today—to witness a virtual garden shop first hand!

Intertwined thoughts of culture and nature inspired me to read Gary Paul Nabhan's *Songbirds, Truffles, and Wolves: An American Naturalist in Italy*. Following Nabhan on his field trip through the Tuscan and Umbrian countryside prompted memories of my father, who had been a farmer, rancher, and agriculture teacher for most of his life.

In grade school I'd marveled at the ribbons and banners on my father's classroom walls, championship honors his students had won in agronomy competitions. In contests of my own making, I too learned to recognize big and little bluestem grass, Indian grass, and side oats grama. And to fulfill requirements for one of my Girl Scout badges, I made botanical "specimen" pages. I sandwiched individual grass samples between sheets of waxed paper, inserted labels for identification, and then pressed them with a warm iron. Following the same procedure, I collected leaves and made pages representing most of the trees on our place: elm, pecan, walnut, sumac, mesquite, cottonwood, redbud, wild plum, blackhaw, mountain laurel, Mexican buckeye, and a variety of oaks. And my fancy for nature paid me back years later when I aced a college botany test, correctly identifying a hundred plants and trees on campus that day. (Would I remembered even a dozen today!)

Last spring in Verona, having recently read Edith Wharton's *Italian Gardens and Their Villas*, I made a point of visiting the Giardino Giusti. Close enough for me to walk from my hotel, it demanded no later than mid-morning arrival to guarantee a soft light for photography. And while Giusti wasn't glamorous or monumental in scale, it certainly had special appeal.

Lemons! Everywhere lemons. Atop pedestals strategically placed about the grounds, huge terra cotta urns of skimpy trees dangled sunny globes the size of tennis balls. Fluorescent-yellow tennis balls! (Could I build a *limonaia* in Texas? To be tacked on to the back of my house?) Dazed by a halo of citrus for the rest of the day, I softly hummed the melody of "Lemon Tree," Peter, Paul, and Mary's hit from the 1960s.

Now, in my own front yard garden, squash is of major concern. Three little mounds of gangly sprouted seeds start drawing attention in a neighborhood accustomed to periwinkles. Evening strollers ask questions and compliment my efforts. Mothers pushing baby carriages stop to coo and stare. And within weeks, my odd little squash seedlings evolve into zucchini monsters. They flaunt flailing succulent arms like mutant appendages in a Spielberg movie.

Yet unlike the Italian bush beans growing inches away, my gigantic zucchini plants load themselves with blooms but never bear fruit. Emerging male blossoms quickly expand into bright yellow trumpets the size of my hand, then fold and wither away, eventually being replaced by new ones. While male flowerings repeat their act with ease, only scattered bulbous beginnings of female flowers appear. In the shadow of dominant male blossoms, the knobby-kneed little girl growths never develop into the beautiful specimen like on my seed package.

Then it struck me—why not eat the blossoms and stop worrying about waiting for produce! Quickly thumbing through cookbooks, I selected a fitting recipe: a simple batter from Carol Field's *In Nonna's Kitchen: Recipes and Traditions from Italy's Grandmothers* (1997). The recipe was called "Salvia Fritta," or fried sage leaves, but fried zucchini blossoms was one of the variations.

Minutes before lunch that day, I carried my wicker basket and kitchen shears down our walkway to gather a pollen-filled harvest at curb side—a half-dozen trumpet-shaped blossoms still open in the late-morning sun. I also snipped a handful of nearby sage to accompany my blossom feast, dipping and frying the sage leaves in the same batter as the golden blossoms.

Like so many other times in my life, I'd waited. And while waiting for zucchini, I'd let baskets of savory blossoms go to waste. From what I've read and witnessed, Italians seldom postpone personal pleasure. They never hesitate to enjoy life at hand. They seduce, induce, invite, squeeze, and pull life from every moment, every hour, each day.

Because of a simple garden experience, my life has new meaning. When life is squat, eat blossoms. Don't wait for the fruit. Plant joy in your life, wear seeds around your neck—and go to Italy as often as you can.

of Italy's pop-music performers (Eros Ramazzotti, Italian "bluesman" Zucchero, Italy's Bob Dylan—Fabrizio de André, or the hypnotic voice of Andrea Bocelli), there's plenty of Italian music to suit my mood. Eros stirs the teen spirit in me, Zucchero appeals to the gypsy blood flowing through my veins, Fabrizio keeps me mellow—and Bocelli? What can I say about Andrea Bocelli that women everywhere haven't already moaned and sighed? Even his name seduces: bo-CHEL-ee, bo-CHEL-ee, bo-CHEL-ee! Infusing shots of romance straight into the bloodstream, his music fast-tracks its way to the heart.

Italian mandolin music and a few odd little tunes also whittle their way inside me. Before I know it, I'm humming or singing, smiling and thinking of Italy. Mary Chapin Carpenter's melody titled "What If We Went to Italy" mesmerizes in such a way. It's a happy, simple song like the ones from childhood, the ones that I chirped all day until I drove my mother crazy. Chirpy little numbers also come from opera. When my mother and ten-year-old niece Leah came to visit a few years ago, I bought tickets for *The Barber of Seville.* It was a first-opera experience for both of them. To my ever inquisitive mother, opera was a total immersion; she absorbed the event like a sponge. But my niece? That was different. Between shifting in her seat to stay awake and voicing a million questions and comments, Leah kept me busy. Her twitching made *my* seat feel lumpy. Her occasional droopy eyelids made *me* yawn. And still, her questions exceeded my depth of opera knowledge!

Leah corrected me right and left, spitting out associated music titles and telling me how to pronounce composers' names. She was repeating scattered details picked up in "music memory" from school, the same school I'd attended as a child, but at which I had learned nothing of opera. How is it that kids know so much these days? And where does the information go? Maybe their feet? (Both my nieces, Leah and her younger sister Lanna, wear shoe sizes I've never heard of!)

The point of the story is that the perky little song we came home with that night lingered like the spray of a skunk. While walking to the car and driving home, while decorating Easter cookies until two in the morning—for the rest of the night and for weeks to come—we kept chiming Figaro's self endorsement: Figaro Figaro, Figaro Figaro—Fi-ga-ro, Fi-ga-ro. We drove ourselves mad with laughter and tears. And without a doubt, it was the most rewarding opera experience of my life. Our shared memory of *The Barber of Seville* will last a lifetime.

My first "live" opera was *Rigoletto*, and I was forty years old—not ten! For years I'd struggled over buying season tickets with the Austin Lyric Opera, but never did. One excuse or another kept popping up. Finally, it was a male vocalist originally from Texas who got me seated for my first performance.

"No way," David said, joking with the vocalist's sister. "Opera singers don't come from Abilene, Texas."

"Just wait. You'll believe me about his voice when you hear him sing at the wedding," Nora said, referring to the wedding of a mutual colleague. "You can apologize to me *after* the ceremony."

And David did eat his words. When he came home after the wedding reception, surprisingly enthusiastic, he dropped two tickets to *Rigoletto* in my lap. "Nora was right about her brother. He really *can* sing. I bought tickets for Saturday night, figuring you'd want to go."

Perhaps it was too good to come true, to think that my husband and I would be going to the opera together, sharing first-time opera the way we had shared first-time love long ago. When it looked like a hacking cough would keep David at home, I called a friend to join me last-minute—my traveling partner in Italy from graduate school years. I was surprised to learn that it was her first opera as well.

Vicariously, through Verdi's *Rigoletto*, Linda and I slipped back in time that evening to reclaim grand moments from our journey: *seizing* our first glimpse of Venice, *inhaling* the architecture of Florence, *hugging* desolate Roman columns at Hadrian's Villa near Tivoli.

It turned out that David's only connection to opera that year was his unexpected interest in Luciano Pavarotti. Ever since seeing a rerun of "The Three Tenors" on PBS, he was hooked. The voices had stunned David, and *he* stunned me. My husband likes Pavarotti? Pavarotti who sings in Italian?

Within days, bizarre music combinations started blasting from David's pickup as he drove through the neighborhood and pulled into our driveway, sitting and waiting for one song to end and another to begin. I'm sure the neighbors thought it was odd—the way he alternated between cassette tapes of Bob Wills, Junior Brown, and "The Three Tenors," his oil-and-water mixture of melody.

After reading the novel *Floria Tosca* by Italian writer Paola Capriolo, my Italy fever was further stoked by the Austin Lyric Opera's offering of *Tosca* last spring. Misjudging my arrival time, I sprinted the few blocks from a parking garage to make it before the lights dimmed. How stupid, I thought, to cut it so close. My first time to finagle a seat near the stage, and I'm running down the street like a bull in Pamplona. Sweaty and Italy-crazed breathless, I collapsed into my seat with seconds to spare.

It wasn't a voice of Maria Callas stature, but the Tosca before me resounded with fervor. Who was this gutsy woman with fire in her belly? This take-charge female who knows what she wants? And how easily she disposes of the disgusting, unscrupulous, and conniving Scarpia.

Surprisingly, however, the closing scene prompted unexpected emotions in me. Instead of being saddened by the suicidal ending—Tosca's leap to her death from atop the walls of Castel Sant' Angelo, I almost laughed out loud. Having been tainted by too much *Tosca* trivia prior to the performance, I kept waiting for Tosca to spring back into view. For I'd recently read that one performer (in another production) had "jumped to her death" by leaping onto a trampoline out of sight. That, unpredictably, she had rebounded like a basketball—bouncing high enough for the audience to see!

I regret not seeing Venice's opera house, Teatro la Fenice, before it burned in January of 1996. Deflated by news of the fire that had gutted the location of Verdi's premiere of *Rigoletto* on March 11, 1851, I placed the tragedy in personal historical perspective—126 years before the day I was married. Ever since the arson-declared catastrophe, I've clipped articles to keep track of the sad situation. Like cheating on a blind date by peeking at photos and a personal biography ahead of time, I developed an emotional attachment to a building I'd never met. Only when I returned to Venice, for the special anniversary trip with David, was I finally introduced. I met my blind date face to face.

Was there much to see? No, very little. Was I disappointed? Not at all. Confident that the scaffolded structure before me was deeper than a first impression, I trusted the great history of events that preceded me—all the grand operas once hissed at and lauded within these now soot-stained walls.

While major differences prevent comparison to La Fenice, Vicenza's Teatro Olimpico is another opera house that allures me. I once read that Teatro Olimpico is to Italy what the original Grand Old Opry is to the United States— an honored stage tradition for performers. Springing to mind at the moment is Cecilia Bartoli. Her *Live in Italy* CD was recorded on stage in Vicenza during June of 1998. The CD's enclosed booklet gives details of Bartoli's appearance, including lyrics in Italian and English. And not knowing enough Italian to eavesdrop in Italy, I find the English translation a blessing. It allows me to sing along, or at least mouth the words! The packaging also encloses a nice mini-poster of the event. And, like a teenager papering her bedroom with posters, I stuck mine on a wall right away.

It appears that Teatro Olimpico is Italy's oldest known indoor, or semi-indoor theater (whether or not a roof existed over the seating area remains a mystery, according to some historians) to recapture the lost legacy of a permanent stage with fixed seating—as with ancient Roman theaters. As one of Andrea Palladio's last architectural works (albeit completed after his death), the theater is known for its excellent acoustical interior, primarily due to its wooden construction. Even the stage's false perspective backdrop was constructed in wood but painted to resemble stone.

For yet another reason, I also hold tender memories of this theater. I remember smiling the first time I saw it in 1988, at how unexpectedly familiar the seating was. It was just like the bleachers in the small-town gymnasiums where I'd played junior and high school basketball. Worn and splintered pine risers, branded with initials carved in secret with pocketknives. Seats sticky with stuck bubble gum, spilled popcorn, and Coke.

Though I'm not a big fan of Anne Rice, her *Cry to Heaven* gripped me with a stranglehold. It's not an ordinary read by any stretch of my imagination. The story of a castrated male soprano from an aristocratic family in eighteenth-century Venice made my eyes bulge. So I can't begin to imagine what it does to male readers. Rice puts the cruel and crude world of the Italian *castrati* in your face. The story clutched me from the start, compelled me to comb library indexes and bookstore shelves, where I finally hit upon another fitting novel, *The Last Castrato*, John Spencer Hill's ripping mystery with a Florentine setting.

Soon afterward, before I could locate still more books on the subject, a friend suggested that I rent a video called *Farinelli*. Like *Cry to Heaven*, this R-rated and subtitled movie unveils the eighteenth-century *castrati* in raw candor—in particular, the overlapping lives of two Italian brothers. One is an opera composer; the other is a famous *castrato* with the stage name of Farinelli. One reviewer called it a film that would make the male audience cringe. I cringed too, knowing how my husband (who has never seen the movie) would react.

The *castrati* phenomenon was prompted in part by the fact that women were mostly barred from public exhibitions in seventeenth-century Europe: the *castrati* supplied high soprano voices, often for female roles. I even read one gender-bending account in which a woman, desperate in her desire to perform in public, pretended to be a male *castrato*. It sounded like an old twist on what it takes to succeed in a "man's" world: a woman wants to *sound* like a woman, but must *dress* like a man and *brag* about castration?

Before flying to New York for a weekend "Italian" fling a few years ago, I checked on the possibility of buying tickets to see Luciano Pavarotti perform in Donizetti's *L'Elisir*

D'Amore. Seeing Pavarotti at the Met would be a heightened Italian experience in Manhattan for me. But after searching the Metropolitan Opera's Web site for ticket status, I realized it was not meant to be—except for the hundreds of people in this world who apparently *plan* their New York flings six months in advance. Sold out. No hint of a ticket at any price.

Disappointment, however, forced me to rethink my dilemma. If I couldn't *see* Pavarotti, then at least I'd try to reserve a ticket for the Met's backstage tour. I'd step onto the stage where the maestro would walk. I'd peep into the dressing room where he would *prepare* for the opera I was going to miss! To share the adventure, I called a friend in Connecticut to join me.

Did you ever have a buddy who always made things right when you got together? Click, click—amazing things happen, luck lands in your lap. Even when years lapse between visits, Beth and I are like that for each other. Every time we join forces, miracles sprout before us—whether we've force-bloomed them or not!

In the middle of a downpour, Beth and I somehow managed to snare a taxi in lower Manhattan to take us to the Met by the appointed tour time. And in spite of the tiny detail that we hadn't been able to secure tour tickets ahead of time (also sold out), available slots opened up for us like Moses parting the Red Sea.

Our caring leader, passionate and well informed about

all aspects of opera, provided the excellent insight of an opera fanatic. He told us of occasions at the old Metropolitan when, following a performance, scenery and costumes were pushed out into the street for lack of storage space. We saw wigs and costumes, stage props and scenery, hidden amplifications of one of the world's leading opera houses. Each word our guide delivered came straight from the heart—the vocabulary of a true opera lover.

"Oh," he said, genuinely saddened by our plight, "you really *don't* have tickets for tonight!"

"No, and we're sick about it," I responded. "This trip was a spur-of-the-moment idea, so it was impossible to get seats."

"Hmm. But there is a way," he said, with a hint of confidence gleeming in his eyes. "Just wait it out until the last moment. Stand out front—not in the lobby—and it's very possible that someone will have tickets to sell. It's worked a number of times for me. Nothing's guaranteed, but you should give it a try."

Beth and I looked at each other and grinned. Why not? All of a sudden, it sounded easy. Already, we'd lucked out by gaining admission for the backstage tour. So who was to say we wouldn't get lucky with *L'Elisir D'Amore* too.

Much earlier than anticipated, and before (we thought) it was time to go stand in the rain, Beth spotted a lone woman waving two tickets in one hand, holding a plaid umbrella in the other. She was a plaid sort of woman, meek and ordinary—not the hawk we'd expected. It looked simple that we should confidently walk up and buy her tickets—as if she were holding them in our names.

Then panic set in. Would the miracle woman disappear before we made it across the plaza? Would someone beat us to her? Would we have enough cash for *two* tickets?

But what looked easy, was easy. Our mild-mannered ticket lady turned out to be a season ticket-holder with a sick husband at home. Our Pavarotti tickets cost Beth and me four dollars *less* than their printed price. And it happened so fast we didn't have to stand in the rain and beg—which would have made a much better story!

When the chandeliers rose at the appointed hour of eight, I focused on the glamour before me. Ignoring my non-designer pantsuit and waterproof loafers, I felt like Cher's character in *Moonstruck*—where she's on a first date at the Met with her fiancé's brother, played by Nicolas Cage. The rising chandeliers were all that I expected and wanted them to be—brilliant starbursts that faded into twinkling fireflies, initiating a shared evening with maestro and mega-personality Luciano Pavarotti. Beth and I had done it again!

CHAPTER TEN

Celebrate with Gelato and Expresso

I can never say no to ice cream. On occasions as frequent as lunar eclipses, I ignore pie, cake, or cookies, but never ice cream. The mere thought of its frosty seduction makes me crazy, causes me to lose control. Far worse, I become sentimental. Any mention of ice cream and I'm back in rural Texas where weekly ice-cream churning was a rite of summer. Or, I'm walking the sunny sidewalks of Florence, where I licked my first gelato—*limone* flecked with lemon peel, tart and sweet. A zestful confetti concoction.

When people reminisce about travel or vacations, foremost they talk about food—eating incredible calamari in Seattle, memorable blue-corn tortillas in Sante Fe, the tastiest barbecue brisket in Austin, Dallas, or Kansas City. Whether the food was empirically best or because it really was the best didn't matter.

Ice cream in Italy is like that for me. Displayed like frozen jewels behind glass, gelati and Florence go together. Gelati is Italy at its best!

Ice-cream making was a usual event when I was a child. Mother's *crème de la crème* was homemade vanilla prepared with local eggs, milk and cream direct from the cow (our own Jersey), and *real* vanilla extract (not the cheap imitation). We also had peach ice cream when fuzzy cling peaches ripened in the summer and banana nut flavor as an alternate treat. Our freezer held a ready supply of native pecans from our land, picked and hulled with brown-stained fingers in the fall, cracked and shelled by hand all winter long.

The ice cream "freezing" process was straightforward.

A desired mixture was first beaten in a bowl, and poured into the freezer's gallon-size canister. The dasher and lid were secured, and the crank mechanism was connected to the dasher stem and locked tight.

Ice soon followed. We froze our own in empty half-gallon milk cartons that were rinsed and saved for this purpose. After peeling the cardboard, we chipped the block of ice and used it to fill the ice-cream maker's cedar bucket to the brim. Rock salt was poured on top and cranking began without hesitation.

My job came next. After layering newspapers on top of the freezer to make an insulated cushion, I sat on it to hold the contraption together—while my brothers, Dwight and Dennis, took turns with the crank arm. Extra ice and salt were added periodically, according to how fast the ice melted. And after half an hour, more or less, when the turning became stiff (indicating the mixture was frozen), it was time to fuss over *who* would lick the dasher, and get the first taste. Finally, after clearing away the ice and salt, Mother removed the plastic lid to extract and award the frozen paddle like a lollipop. Then, she scooped soft-frozen dips from the stainless steel canister still sitting in a slushy brine.

During the week, I also licked ice cream cones after school, stopping daily to visit Jim and Deana's Cafe on our tiny town square. Holding my breath in anticipation, I watched Deana dig deep into my favorite cardboard canister behind the counter. She perched a pink strawberry ball on my cone with precision.

But even better were the times when cigar-chewing Jim escaped from the kitchen to dip ice cream for me—two scoops for my dime! With a clipped bow tie dangling from one corner of his starched white collar, he balanced two monstrous mounds on top of a cone, patting them down hard so they wouldn't fall off. With loose clumps hovering above my hand, I acted with a degree of emergency to lick, nibble, and expertly carve the frozen beast to manageable size—before safely pushing my way out the swinging screen door. And though Jim did the same kind deed for lots of kids in town, he always made *me* feel special, like I was the only child deserving of a double dip that day.

At home, we also spooned store-bought "mellorine" throughout the year, from rectangular cartons with folded and leaky end flaps. We filled skyscraper glasses with the vanilla-flavored spongy stuff and poured Coke, Big Red, or Orange Nesbitt soda pop on top. Concocting foamy frosted "floats," we satisfied our ice-cream cravings until the *real* stuff cranked its way into our lives again.

To the point of obsession (like me), Italians love ice cream. Their tradition of consuming chilled drinks and desserts appears to have evolved from centuries of snow and ice gathering. According to Elizabeth David, in her book *Harvest of the Cold Months: A Social History of Ice and Ices*, the ice trade in Italy was documented as early as the fifteenth century.

But who invented gelati? Who created ice cream as we know it today?

Searching further, I found the answer more complicated than I'd imagined. While Elizabeth David accepts the probability that southern Italian *sorbetti* were based on oriental precedents, she attributes the city of Naples with being the probable home of artificial freezing techniques. Evidently, the procedure was first discovered in the sixteenth century, but not fully explored and used until perhaps as late as the mid-seventeenth century.

Numerous sources also recognize Naples as the birthplace of gelati vending, the self-corrupting but divine institutions known as ice-cream parlors—the yin and yang of sweet indulgence.

Though a definitive date for ice cream's origin remains unclear, it also remains unimportant—at least to me. I accept on faith, no matter its place in history, that a market-clever Neapolitan created gelati, and I'm forever in his debt! It's enough for me to know that the fine art of ice-cream making was *perfected* in Italy.

Like an arrest-me-red Ferrari in a speed trap, some kinds of gelati stand out above others. Italy's astonishing fruit flavors demand multiple sampling, one dip at a time—*gelato di melone* (like eating pureed frozen cantaloupe with cream and sugar), also *limone, pesca, fragola,* and *frutti di bosco.* Or, *gelato di albicocca,* my chosen fruit pleasure—apricot!

Non-fruit offerings are equally sinful. My husband's preferred flavor is *gelato di stracciatella*, a rich vanilla ice cream with shavings and broken slivers of pure Swiss chocolate. In every city he visited, and in a strictly "un-Italian" manner, David requested *due* dips of his favorite by pointing two fingers at his canister of choice. And when puzzled servers questioned his selection for two dips alike, he pointed again to confirm. It appears that Italians prefer at least two kinds of ice cream on their cones, one stacked on top of the other—never two dips of the same old thing.

Traveling alone in Lucca a year later, I finally hit upon my own exceeds-all-others favorite: a two-flavor act discovered after a scant million calories of Tuscan research. The exalted winner is a combo-creation, tested and sanctioned on repeated occasions. (I had to be sure!) Four times in one day is my record so far—a double cone for breakfast and again as a mid-morning snack, two dips at lunch, and snow-capped twin peaks during the *passeggiata*, my evening stroll.

But next time I'll go for broke—*five* double dips in a day. When next in Lucca, straight from the train and still toting my bag I'll march like a sugar ant to the heavenly *gelateria* that offers my coveted, albeit nutty, combination—one dip of *mandorla* neighbored with one dip of *pinolata*. Almond and pine nut!

While *sorbetti* and *granite* also deserve recognition, gelati is the link that connects me to what I know best—pure, sweet ice cream to be licked on a cone, or eaten from a cup with a baby spoon in Lucca. And nothing but ice cream can diminish the summer heat while standing in line to climb the three-hundred-plus stone steps to the top of Florence's grand *duomo* for a bird's-eye view of the city of gelati.

A few years ago in Milan, on the parting night of our twentieth-anniversary adventure, I drank a microscopic cup of espresso—my first ever, at home or abroad. I had already consummated a sumptuous affair with pasta and seafood, followed by a shared slice of *torta di cioccolata*, a sinful chocolate cake. Then, in final tribute to a country I adore, but to David's dismay, I impulsively ordered a last-minute cup of "Italian coffee," an espresso—when *he* was ready to leave.

Never a coffee drinker myself, I'd expected the flavor to be bitter and overwhelming, but it surprised me. Sweetened with sugar and rich with frothy chocolate-colored *crema*, my first espresso was smooth and delicious.

Only later did it hit me that I'd doped myself with megatons of caffeine. My innocent-looking *toy* cup of *crema*-topped seduction kept David and me both awake all night.

Earlier in the evening, we'd worried that a barking dog below our balcony would interrupt our sleep. But not a problem—he only barked once. Instead, I was the demon puppy dog with espresso pumping through my veins. Bouncing on the mattress like a child on a new trampoline, I flipped and flopped and dove into the ocean of our bed. I splashed and undulated vibrating waves—no coins required. Finally, at four in the morning, my wiggles relaxed and I drifted on calmer waters.

In public or private, *caffè* or *cucina*, espresso drinking is entrenched in the daily lives of Italians. Their passion for coffee is especially evident during early morning hours when the locals drop in at the same tiny bar day after day to "make" *colazione*—enjoy a stand-up breakfast of espresso and a pastry.

While various guidebooks confirm that Europe's first coffeehouse opened in Venice in the seventeenth century, it's the eighteenth-century Florian on the Piazza San Marco that is the city's oldest *caffè* establishment. Popularized by Henry James' description in *The Aspern Papers* and by Katherine Hepburn's escapades in her *Summertime* movie, the Florian induces seductive thoughts of the past. It's impossible not to think about the people who sat there before you.

The first time I splurged on a refreshment at one of the little Florian tables on the *piazza*, near the grand piano, I suddenly became Katherine Hepburn waiting for Rossano Brazzi. I fell hopelessly romantic and sappy—aroused by the music and the moment. I never thought I would fall for the fantasy, but I did. As I caressed the silver serving tray with its banded rope edge, my heart fluttered and lost rhythm. As I sipped a tobacco-colored espresso from the tiny cup with its blue and gold insignia, I felt guilty, as if I were cheating on my husband. Expecting *my* stranger to arrive!

Ride a Bicycle at Home and on Tour

P er capita, more Italians than Americans own cars. When a news article charted this comparison a few years ago, it shocked me. Beyond its flashy sports car image, Italy appears to have a fetish for the ordinary too—all kinds of cars. And like many Europeans, but unlike most Americans, Italians also enjoy two-wheeled conveyances, riding motorcycles and bicycles.

A few years ago in Vicenza, David and I entertained ourselves for hours watching local citizens transport themselves and their goods on assorted *bicicletti*. The abundance of casual pedaling intrigued and surprised us, and we envied their unhurried pace. Who were these people and where were they going? How did their lives differ from our own? Should *we* be riding bicycles more often in *our* daily lives?

Dining alfresco, savoring *prosciutto* and *Asagio panini* and guzzling Texas size bottles of *acqua naturale*, David and I perched like pigeons on basilica steps, cooing and observing puzzled pathways as bicycles crisscrossed the city center. Businessmen wandered along in coats and ties with daily newspapers folded over handlebars. Fashionably heeled businesswomen coursed their way across the *piazza* with skirts shifted high. Bicycling moms jingled bells to clear paths while toting their new offspring in body slings. Leisurely grandmothers pedaled by with overloaded baskets of vegetables, crusty breads, and gladiolus stems a mile long. Nuns drifted along with their billowing habits, looking like sails on Lake Como.

In the Swiss Alps traveling toward Italy, Edith Wharton, in her travel memoir *Italian Backgrounds*, once wrote about a scene she observed following dinner one evening. Her brief depiction of a bicycle-owning Italian chef is memorable.

> Dinner over, the eager spectators, hastening to the terrace (with a glimpse, as they pass the vaulted kitchen, of the Italian *chef* oiling his bicycle amid the débris of an admirable meal) . . . .

I love the image of the chef oiling his bicycle "amid the débris of an admirable meal." My reaction to the scene was to laugh and ask, "Was he oiling his bicycle with olive oil?"

Italian cycling, or *ciclismo*, is practiced and appreciated by all ages. Devoted race fans wait for hours to see their heroes flash by in faint whirls of recognition. Two major competitions, the Milan-San Remo (typically held in March) and the Giro d'Italia (typically held in May), are newsworthy traditions. Thousands of people line the routes for these performances in clear testimony that Italians are wild about cycling. Italian Mario Cipollini's sexy profile in the sport and Italian Marco Pantani's win of the Giro d'Italia *and* the Tour de France in 1998 further clinched cycling's popularity in Italy for years to come. Pantani's homecoming that year was a national celebration.

Only Greg LeMond and Texan Lance Armstrong have fostered comparable cycling excitement in the States. Armstrong, a "favorite son" among Italian racing fans (because of the respect Armstrong has shown for deceased Italian rider Fabio Casartelli), has quadrupled the visibility of bicycling as a serious sport in Texas. And Armstrong's mighty feat of winning the 1999 Tour de France, after rebounding from testicular cancer, is astonishing to say the least!

In contrast, Americans more typically interpret Italian transportation as sporty cars and motorcycles, not bicycles. We jump-start to thoughts of handling a Ferrari, Maserati, Lamborghini, or Alfa Romeo. We admire Lyle Lovett's Ducati motorcycle as the sexiest, albeit affluent,

Italian toy of choice for midlifers seeking two-wheeled adventure. We're seduced by thoughts of mindless weekend getaways on Italian *motorini*: a bold Piaggio that scoots us to our destination, or a classic Velocifero that putters us off into the countryside to escape our cities. We quickly forget the mosquito-buzzing swarms of vespas the last time we visited Florence, but remember, clearly, how Audrey Hepburn buzzed the Colosseum on a scooter in *Roman Holiday*. Or we relive romantic scenes from *Rome Adventure*—Troy Donahue zipping off with Suzanne Pleshette to tour the sites via motorbike.

Classic Ferrari red or not, however, an Italian sports car is a luxury that exceeds my countrified comprehension. Likewise, the idea of buying a reproduction 1950s Velocifero (like the real one in the Museum of Modern Art's permanent design collection in New York, and available a few years ago in a Neiman Marcos catalog) holds little appeal. In truth, all manner of *motorized* speed demons escape me. Why ride a noisy "weed trimmer on wheels" into the quiet dewdrop moments of the Italian *campagna*? Give me a whispering Italian bicycle instead—sunny yellow like a yellow-checkered cab, sturdy and bold. A *bicicletta* that reminds me of a sun-drenched and leisurely Italy.

For now, I've settled on "Italianizing" my sleepy old American bike, a contraption that's more turtle than rabbit. To my husband's horror (he rides a *real* bicycle), I traded in my skinny hard saddle for a wide cruiser seat with creaking springs. Next, I mounted a big shopping basket—an attractive bag-lady-on-wheels appearance for me. And I added a tiny silver bell that makes a musical "ding." (People turn and expect ice cream.) Forthcoming is a mudguard (Italian women are spotless—not one speck of mud on the back of their legs) and a mountable light that will beam me home after dark.

In sophisticated contrast, my spouse rides a blue Tommasini bought secondhand in Austin. Since I was the one crazy about Italy, not him, his unexpected purchase of an Italian bicycle both surprised and delighted me. But David was also excited and proud of his "new" treasure. Even used, it cost more than any bike he'd ever owned.

So why was I shocked to find this pedal-powered vehicle parked in the house without a permit? There it was, leaning against the chairs in our library-dining room, alongside other valued possessions, our books. The garage, according to I-can-hear-it-now predictions, was either too hot, too cold, too dirty, or too far away.

Hmm. Should I ticket him on the spot? Or call a wrecker to haul it away?

Then, I remembered my own previous "parking violations." For twenty years, following us like a white elephant in tow every time we moved (too many houses to count), a bulky, four-harness floor loom was stationed in the middle of our living room—before I finally relegated it to a garage, seldom having used it at all. At least David *rides* his bicycle. I never once wove a rug!

As long as he didn't paint stripes on the floor to designate private parking, I decided it best to accept the situation without fuss. After all, the bicycle *was* Italian.

Seduced by my handsome new housemate, the blue Tommasini, I secretly fondled its sleek profile, running my hands along its contours, stroking its skinny saddle seat. Sexiness aside, I couldn't wait to unravel details of an Italian heritage. Who? What? Where was it made? I wanted to know more.

When I had first conjured the whim of an anniversary trip to Italy, I used David's bicycle as bait, to lure and hook a reluctant-to-travel husband: "Wouldn't you like to go to Italy to see where your bike was made?" On the flip side, my underhanded means of coaxing him to travel meant fulfilling my end of the bargain: learning about the city of Grosseto, home of the Tommasini factory and showroom, located southwest of Siena near the coastal edge of Tuscany.

Our base location for exploring the Tuscan region (including Grosseto) was Siena. But first we had to get there. After arriving in Milan, we chugged south by train to spend our first night in La Spezia—in a hotel near the train station. Italy Rail tickets provided us with primary transportation. Everywhere else we walked. No rental car. No taxis.

After La Spezia, we headed to our Sienese destination, via Pisa and tiny Empoli, catching glimpses of the region along the way. Already, my auto-focusing camera was happy and humming, content in capturing vague, blurry images through open train windows.

A few days later, the train trip to Grosseto also proved perfect for open-window photography. We practically had an entire car to ourselves. While David hunkered on one side next to the windows, I plopped myself down on the opposite side of the train, poised and ready to shoot slides. As the track curved in and out, the sun danced in on one side, then the other. David scouted for approaching villas and farmhouses within his view, alerting me to the best of what he saw. Meanwhile, I bounced back and forth, side to side and seat to seat, seeking the best angle, trying to see all.

Like a border collie riding in a pickup, I poked my head (and camera) out one window, then another. I sucked in for tunnels and passing trains while the wind glued my eyelashes to my forehead. My tongue hung out so I could pant and drool properly. I barked at the sites. I did everything except wag my tail. Or maybe I did that too.

Mr. Tommasini's daughter, Barbara, picked us up at the train station. Her reply to my fax from the States had been gracious, hospitable beyond imagination. Had her father not been at a trade show in Milan that day, I'm sure David would have been "measured" for a new road bike—a sporty yellow TecnoLight or Velocista, a custom frame proportioned and scrutinized by Signor Irio Tommasini himself. Instead, after having toured the facility, David set off on a bike ride toward the sea at Castiglione della Pescaia while Barbara treated me to a city tour, within the old Roman walls of Grosseto.

Later, I gloated over getting David to the factory without mishap, supremely pleased with myself that things had turned out so well. Yet, in truth, I knew better; it had little to do with me. The secret of our success was the kindness and generosity of the people we had met. The Tommasini factory welcomed us in spite of our excessive boasting (we take Texas with us wherever we go!) and despite our asking a million questions. Texas drawl and all, we offered respect and common courtesy, and it was returned to us ten-fold in true Italian hospitality.

People who walk and ride bicycles experience the best of Italy. Cars and trains go too fast.

"Guess what I saw while riding my bike this morning?" David teased one afternoon. And without letting me respond, he continued, "Workers picking grapes!" He knew this would floor me, and it did.

"You've got to be kidding. Where did you go!" I couldn't believe the luck he'd had on his first outing in Siena. Instantly pouting, knowing David had carried no camera, I knew the moment was lost. I'd missed it—missed getting *close* to the grapes. All the vines I'd seen so far had been from a speeding train.

"It's not very far from here. You'd be surprised. Just a few miles out—four or five. We'll rent you a bike and go back tomorrow." I couldn't believe my ears. My heart pounded at the prospect.

Then I worried. "Are you sure I can do it? How big are these hills and how many will I have to climb?" My legs were okay for flat stretches of road, but pedaling uphill was a different matter. Prior to our trip I'd worried about making arrangements for a bicycle for David, and yet hadn't considered riding one myself. I hadn't absorbed the implication of Italy's hill-town reputation, until now.

Strutting like a rooster after riding his first bicycle in Italy, David was actually elated about riding steep hills. Before arriving, he'd fretted about the "mountains" he'd expected to find. Yet so far, he was pleased to find biking in this part of Tuscany to be tolerable. Most of the inclines had been similar to or only slightly worse than the ones he tackled in Austin.

But could I ride the hills? Sure, sure. And would it kill me? Maybe. But I knew I had to try. Even if it meant wearing out body parts (some too personal to mention), I knew I'd do anything to see grapes being harvested in Italy. Then it struck me: What would I wear? I'd seen the *brute* that would be my mount, with its saddle no more than a skinny strip of leather!

So when David generously offered to loan me a spare pair of *his* padded bicycle shorts, I accepted without challenge. The timing was not right for poking fun at my husband's compulsive over-packing disorder. He'd simply reverse the situation anyhow: "Didn't pack enough clothes?" He'd never let me forget that I had borrowed some of his in Italy. But for now, it didn't matter. At the moment, all I could think of was my tailbone. My ego would have to wait.

When David warned me about Siena's traffic being heavy, he was right. Yet he was also on target about Sienese drivers being courteous. I never feared being bumped off the road, as was so often the case at home. The fact that most of the locals were driving small cars helped matters, but more important and convincing was their attitude.

David hung back to let me set an easy pace. I stopped often to shoot pictures: rolling plowed fields and faded sunflowers, clustered stone buildings and silver olive groves, patchwork panorama views. Country *alberghi* mixed with farmhouses and working farms called *fattorie*.

"They're *still* picking grapes!" I shouted to David as I topped a gentle rise. I'd worried it would all be gone—grapes, pickers, equipment, everything—like a vanishing vapor without hint of a residue.

The crew closest to us were resting, wiping their brows and laughing, looking at us looking at them; we smiled and nodded hello. The other pickers were harder to distinguish among the distant rows of vines, but they all *looked* like women. Were the only male pickers the ones near the road—the workers enjoying a siesta?

Continuing farther, David repeatedly commented on how nice it was to feel free on the road, like you belonged there—no threats from honking pickups or from cyclonic winds when larger trucks whizzed by within inches. "It's nice the way Italian drivers respect bicycles," he said. "You'd never see this happen in Texas!"

Several miles later and ready to turn around, we stopped to rest under fig trees that shaded the road. Like Eve, I was overwhelmed by the sudden temptation to partake of forbidden fruit. Only a few succulent-looking figs were ripe enough to eat, but that was enough—one for David, one for me.

Upon biting into the seeded morsel, I lapsed into memories of the old fig trees next to my granddaddy's iron-forging shed years ago. The trees there grew tall and bushy enough to cover the entire north side of the building. Stiff, fan-shaped leaves provided deep shade and seclusion—a cool playing spot, and good cover for hiding from older brothers.

In Vicenza, David and I also rode bicycles together. At the train station, we located an ample supply of red city bikes with fat seats, kickstands, and mudguards—marked with the identification: COMUNE DI VICENZA. They were well maintained and offered at reasonable rental rates.

David left his Texas driver's license as deposit for our two cruisers and we were on our way.

Following a path he'd tested the day before, we entered a bike lane near the Villa Rotonda, and across from a *pasticceria*—likewise spotted and sampled on David's previous ride. We sampled now and called it breakfast, a sticky-finger banquet of apricot- and custard-filled pastries.

The lane was adjacent to a well-traveled road, with cornfields on either side that yielded *granturco*—North American maize imported by Columbus—used to make the region's famous polenta dishes. Beyond the cornfields, the paved bike route veered from the main road and followed a meandering path behind scattered houses and buildings, headed toward a village. Where necessary, we slowed to navigate the offset barricades that prohibited cars and mopeds.

We pedaled past flower gardens, vegetable patches, orchards, and scattered vineyards—all faded by the passing of summer. Plowed fields, vacant factories, old lonely mills. Local riders dallied in the gentleness of a Sunday afternoon: parents riding with small children; individuals cycling for exercise and sun-ripened pleasure; elderly couples riding bikes, side by side and holding hands.

Seeking deeper exposure into the countryside, we quit the public bike trail and followed a series of two-lane, then single-lane, paved roads farther into the *campagna* in the general direction of Padua and Venice. We crossed a narrow bridge where a nearby wooden waterwheel lifted scoops of water from an old millpond, while a cathedral spire pierced the horizon—as picturesque as any postcard.

At a fork in the road, we paused to admire a free-standing pedimented shrine with a figure of Mary. Artificial and fresh flowers and handmade offerings filled its niche. The altar's unexpected presence beside the road reminded me of how Frances Mayes described the shrine near her beloved Bramasole in *Under the Tuscan Sun.* Curious like Mayes (I might have passed without notice had I not read her book), I wanted to know something about the people who deposited and tended the items in this sacred niche. What was their connection to this honored place along the roadway?

Continuing, we soon came upon a dirt and gravel road that led to an old stone villa, a symmetrical two-story structure elongated to each side with one-story wings. Except for a few lingering grape clusters from recently plucked vines flanking the main drive, the place looked neglected, deserted. Stopping long enough to click a quick picture, I knew this place would draw me closer. On the way back, I was sure to stop again.

Less than a mile down the road, an asymmetrical farm-house with fenced pens and side yards formed a casual compound in contrast to the villa. Peeling pink stucco encased a structure that was house and barn all in one, sitting perpendicular and close to the road, with shuttered windows on the end that resembled a house.

The yard and grounds were scattered with old farm equipment, scratching roosters and hens, pecking ducks, roaming cats, and one sleepy dog. Stone, board, and wire fences indicated a medley of domesticated animals. Raised hutch-like shelters made me think of rabbits.

Climbing roses nudged the fence along the road, and late summer tomatoes joined scant zucchini blossoms in dotting color into an otherwise tranquil still life. Empty and flower-filled pots and metal tubs partially lined a gravel area where two small cars were parked askew. From the open lower windows on the road end of the farmhouse, muffled and chattering noises spilled onto the pavement where we straddled our bikes—while a local family gathered for *pranzo*, their midday meal.

On the other side of the road sat a smaller one-story house, also with fenced enclosures of varying proportion and purpose. Looking odd and seemingly out of place with its peeling blue paint (the bold color surprised me), the structure fronted the road where an overburdened apple tree bowed from the weight of ripened red fruit. Encircling below, a layer of fallen apples covered the ground like a Christmas tree skirt.

Unfortunately, the small cluster of buildings signaled a turnaround spot for us—time to head back.

Retracing our path, I was anxious to see more of the stone villa that had earlier tweaked my curiosity. When it came into view, I was pulled like a dousing rod bending toward water. Insisting that we inspect up close, I led David down a side lane that turned to run parallel with the building's facade before connecting to the central driveway. It was a perfect opportunity to see a centuries-old country villa firsthand, while staying on open and unposted land.

As we rode closer, the architectural details revealed vestiges of a regal life—rusticated stonework, heavily shuttered windows, carved statuary within and on top of a pediment that crowned the central block. Under a glaring afternoon sun, the shadowy mildew and rust stains on the cold gray stone were grave-like, lifeless—yet endearing to me. But when we stopped our bikes in front of the structure to discuss its condition, clanking dinner plates and utensils rattled life into the air. Our seemingly abandoned villa was not dead at all, not lifeless *inside*. On the other side of sad, decaying walls and under the broken tiles of a clay-clad roof, food was being cooked and consumed. Struck by the sounds of the living, we launched a silent escape.

Yet departure down the grapevine-lined corridor tempted me as the fig trees had near Siena. Instead of immediately trailing David to the main road, I lingered and started scanning for grapes, looking for a single lonely bunch missed by pickers.

Finally I saw it—one perfect plump cluster, hanging like candy before me. In much the same way that I used to ride my horse, Brownie, under wild grapevines to pick grapes as a child, I eased my bicycle beneath the targeted fruit at the edge of the road. Sanctioning my action by telling myself "the harvest is over," I pulled on the stem expecting magic. For a moment at least, I was standing in the trellised grape arbor I'd always dreamed of. When nothing happened, I yanked harder. Still the cluster held tight. Its cord of life was thicker and tougher than any grape stem I had ever tried to break.

With no time to dig out my Swiss army knife, I stripped a handful of sweetness instead. Proud of the smashed plunder dripping from my hand, I crammed what I could in my mouth as adrenaline fueled my getaway. Spitting seeds right and left along the way, I hurried to catch up with my partner.

David knew nothing of my wayward undertaking— until he saw me. Then he laughed. And in his usual way of responding to me, my husband slowly shook his head without saying a word.

Denial was impossible. Like a calico cat with feathers in her mouth, my juice-stained shirt said it all. And with fingers stuck tight to a sticky handlebar, there was only one thing left to do. I licked my lips *con brio* and purred a confession of sin.

Contemplate the Art and Architecture of Italy

The day I realized the depth of my passion for Italy was a day of celebration. That evening when David came home from work, I met him at the door bursting with good news: "I've decided to write a book about Italy!"

With traffic-stopping enthusiasm for the notion, my husband responded, "I think I'll go for a bike ride."

"Writing about Italy is right for me," I said. "Italy will be my first book."

"The sun won't go down for a couple of hours," he said. "There's still plenty of time for me to ride."

"And Italy brings my love of architecture into perspective," I continued. "I finally have direction for my writing."

"It'll only take a couple of minutes to change clothes," David added, before disappearing down the hall and around a corner.

"I want to write about all kinds of ways to feed my fever for Italy," I persisted, raising my voice to penetrate a wall. "Fun things to do *before* a trip—Italian-inspired activities."

"Have you seen my helmet?" said David, reappearing like a Superman act.

"I want to write about craving pasta and Puccini opera and books and movies about Italy. About using an Italian pen to write on Florentine paper while listening to mandolin music."

Then Superman flew downstairs and I followed like Lois.

"One tire looks a little low. I'd better grab a spare tube."

"I'll make it a how-to book and call it *14 Ways to Satisfy Your Love Affair with Italy.*"

"Thanks, but I don't need sunscreen today." I hadn't offered, but David knows it's my habit to remind him.

"If I pursue this book, it'll mean sacrifices. I want to concentrate on writing for a while and start saying *no* to paying clients."

"If you get hungry, don't wait on me. Go ahead and eat supper."

"But what about the book? Do you think it's a good idea?"

"I'll be back about 8:30," said David, as he rolled his Tommasini from its parking spot beside the dining room table, out the front door, and down the sidewalk. Then he turned to me and added, "Yes, I think it's great. Go ahead and write your book. But why don't you write about books and movies and opera and gelato—all that Italian stuff you're so crazy about?"

I wanted to throw a shoe, but decided it was smarter to applaud *his* advice. "Thanks for the suggestion," I chirped. "What a wonderful idea!" Too bad I didn't get it recorded on tape, as proof of his support later on.

It was classic "he said, she said." Instead of communication newlywed-style, we were talking in marital telepathy, a condition that develops after twenty years of marriage. Speed-reading my spouse like a well-thumbed novel, I could read between the lines. I knew David supported me, *believed* in me, and that was all I needed.

Prior to solidifying a balanced focus for my writing, before realizing Italy seduced me in more ways than architecture, I had considered writing a book called *Palladio Fever*. After all, the sixteenth-century architect Andrea Palladio had enticed me long ago with his villas, *palazzi*, and grand public buildings in the Veneto region. Already, I'd visited a few of the monumental works that had guided Thomas Jefferson at Monticello. I'd witnessed the physical world of late-Renaissance Italy and recognized its hand on the 1888 Texas Capitol—a building dear to my soul, precious to many Texans.

Most people know a little about Palladio whether they realize it or not. His influence on Western architecture is everywhere, visible in both the grand and the ordinary. His antiquity-inspired presence and authority in English architecture is unquestionable. And in the United States, Palladianism assumes the familiar regal form of classical domes and temple fronts on courthouses and capitol buildings.

In frightful contrast, stateside *residential* builders and developers also lay claim to this famous architect by building and boasting homes with "Palladian windows"—any arch-topped window appears to qualify. It's a pet peeve of mine. How dare they associate my beloved Palladio with their cheesy plastic and metal frames—glued on facades like postage stamps stuck on letters! Where's the depth of character, the honesty?

Museums and cathedrals attract me, but hoards of people scare me away. When there's a line with a head count of, say, *two*, I move on. So my experience in Venice's Church of San Zaccaria was a fluke, a novelty, a rendezvous with art void of crowds.

With few bodies stirring in the heat of the afternoon siesta, it looked easy that I should quietly slip through the heavy front doors and admire one of Bellini's grand Venetian altarpieces in peace. I longed to be surrounded by the cool darkness of stone walls, not guidebook-toting tourists.

But inside, a bright light glowed like a search beam. *No*, it was a half-dozen lights, directed rays. Focused radiation on tripods. I had walked in on a photo shoot, a professional photography session for Giovanni Bellini's *Madonna with Saints*. In place of dark somber hues, as perceived in ordinary *chiesa* lumens, the colors of the painting were bold and polished: heart-stopping reds, opulent ultramarine blues, saturated and illuminated golds. Resting on a nearby pew, I contemplated the Bellini masterpiece and absorbed the well-timed "brilliance" of my visit—for the few minutes it lasted.

Next time around, in Venice, Florence, or possibly Rome, art will take higher ground. (I realize what I'm missing!) I'll suck up the courage to queue and go into museums I've not entered in years and institutions I've never entered at all. I'll load up on bottled water and pack a good book on art, then grab a double gelato before staking my position in line.

Yet before leaving home the next time, I'll re-read Robert Hellenga's novel called *The Sixteen Pleasure*s. It's a book conservator's nightmare with twists and turns, a saga about priceless art being salvaged by "mud angels" when the Arno River flooded Florence in 1966. Then, I'll sit down at my computer for virtual museum tours of exquisite Italian art—from Bellini to Veronese, via Internet.

With each trip to Italy I expect to write *volumes* of mind-boggling notes about Roman and Renaissance art and architecture. With each voyage I think I'll pen copius notes to accompany the slew of slides that I shoot.

Without doubt, I intend to create poetic and inventive essays while visiting *tour de force* examples of architecture: the Pantheon's exemplary spherical dome in Rome, Palazzo Farnese's definitive semicircular stairs in Caprarola, eminent models of Roman civilization at Hadrian's Villa near Tivoli. Without question, I plan to give birth to lofty compositions on time-honored principles extracted from Renaissance artists—Alberti's rules on perspective, Mantegna's archeological inspirations, Boticelli's mythological interest, Da Vinci's *sfumato* technique, Titian's command of color.

But, somehow, it never happens that way. I never come home with eloquent and bountiful pages of prose about art and architecture. Instead, when I unpack my bag, gather my spiral notebooks, and read them, I discover lavish scribbled entries about toilets and bathrooms!

I've often asked myself, "How does this happen?" Does my brain slip gears once my feet land in Italy? Does the listmaker, me, turn suddenly aimless? What happens to the fertile collection of *intelligent* notes I'd intended to produce? Where's the teeming data I'd counted on using to write articles for submission to academic journals? Where's the abundance of creative cultural reflections I'd calculated on having to write thought-provoking essays—the pensive words people read on the last pages of magazines?

I can't submit commentary on Italian bathroom minutiae to *The New Yorker*, *Smithsonian Magazine*, or *The New York Times Magazine*. Or can I?

If anyone were to ask, I'd declare "the Italian bathroom experience" to be a classic Italian moment. It's comparable to the experience of watching Italians talk with their hands (or, these days, talking to themselves until you notice the cell phones) or whittle their way through a crowd on a vespa. In each case, you have to see it to believe it!

During our anniversary trip a few years ago, classic showering adventures were reinforced on numerous occasions. Stepping out and into a puddle any duck would appreciate made me realize in La Spezia why Italian hotel proprietors provide bath *sheets*, not hankerchief-looking towels. Wisely, I've decided, sheeting is provided that is big enough to dry a person's body *and* the floor where that person stands! Still, each time I hesitate. Each time I'm reluctant to wipe the soupy floor with a starched and ironed piece of cloth. Wouldn't this look nice on a table instead?

When David and I first checked into our room in Siena, the second night of our special trip, we were charmed by the presence of an updated sophisticated-looking shower. The stall was a capsule of glass, sleek in its appearance, the way Italian furniture is spare with simple lines. It looked promising, like it was capable of providing a pleasant body-laundering experience. However, since looks so often mislead, I shouldn't have been surprised with the shower's inability to function. But I was.

The only way to enter the glass chamber was by way of toilet—stepping over it. The door opened in the wrong direction and the tolerance between shower and toilet was "barely clears." Inside the contraption was a built-in bidet. Pretty cool, I thought, until I realized the control knobs for this clever auto-douche machine were on the opposite side of the glass from where I stood naked. One had to be a contortionist to reach out and around the stall to start and stop the jet of water. How convenient! If for no other reason, I concluded, at least it afforded the user the opportunity to dump more water on the deck—the obvious explanation for why I've never seen a dirty bathroom floor in Italy.

The overall diameter of the enclosure was also problematic. It was arms up or arms down, nothing in-between. None of this business of sticking your limbs out to the side for routine inspection. Bathing in this shower was the equivalent of showering in a test tube. Or, rather, what I *imagine* showering in a test tube would be like. I've never really done it, you know—soaped myself up in a laboratory experiment.

Then I dropped my razor. Dropping any object that required retrieval—razor, soap, shampoo—was simply not an option in this Sienese water trap. For when I bent over to rescue my disposable Schick, my backside struck the wall behind me like a rear-end collision. Deflected forward, I then smashed my nose smack-dab into more glass. "Where's the air bag?" I pleaded.

It's in predicaments like this when I usually give up and resort to a routine I like to call the "Italian leg shave": the quick passing of a razor over the *inside* of one's legs, slicing bumps off goosebumps in the process. I shave the least possible area that allows me to sleep without stuffing three pillows between my legs, to separate one prickly-pear limb from the other. The rest of my stubble is saved for a tub later on.

In case you haven't detected, I'm a "tub" person. I like deep sloshy vats of steaming water, scalding liquid that forces submersion in sequential order. One set of toes, then the other (lifted in and out a few times like a spoon in a hot bowl of soup). Half-squatting comes next, alternated with one-leg stances that make me look like a pink flamingo. Ouch! Ouch! Will I ever be able to sit?

I hate showers and will do almost anything to avoid one. Yet, in a second I'll gladly relinquish the luxury of soaking, booking any cheap room that's available, tub or not—if that's what it takes to go to Italy without notice.

But I wasn't the only goggle-eyed person when we landed our tricky *closet* in Vicenza. As David entered our hotel chamber he turned livid. "There's no shower, no tub. Just a toilet and a sink!" he exploded. "And the toilet paper's soggy—I checked."

Surveying the situation, I stepped the one step up into the designated cubicle to take a look. "What do you mean there's no shower?" I said. "The whole four-foot square is a waterworks. Didn't you see the shower head on the wall and the drain in the floor?"

For the price of one, we had it all, efficiency in one tidy package: sink, mirror, toilet, shower, *and* wet toilet paper. Oh—and a door. The hinged closure was our only defense against sleeping on soggy linens.

My solitary night's stay in Pisa one spring also afforded a bathroom surprise. But this time, to my delight, my companion was a handsome porcelain steeping tub, not an ugly lowlife shower. It was the largest private bathroom of my trip. I had only one complaint.

Following typical European mode, my disrobed figure and the Pisan bathing gondola were about as ergonomically in sync as a whale in a fishbowl. Where it was narrow, I was not. Where I was dumpy, it was skinny!

Please believe me. Overall, I'm more than thankful for the starched linen toweling and the spotless sanitized tile that come with Italian bathrooms in general. Even low-rated hotels and *pensioni* are immaculate in my experience. Cleanliness aside, however, bathing in Italy is always a challenge. And, in a jocular diversion of hit-or-miss, it's never boring with toilets—this business of flushing, where you must figure out if you should push, pull, turn, crank, or step on a pedal. Not boring at all, but probably not essay material either!

My craving for architecture, especially *old* houses, developed during graduate school. Until then, I knew little of Frank Lloyd Wright, or McKim, Meade and White, and even less about Andrea Palladio. I'd never toured grand homes of identifiable style, never occupied a dwelling that claimed architectural features. Oddly, only one *old* house was remarkable to me as a child.

One lonely structure, located south of the town where I grew up, was both mansion and fortress to me. Its sad yet endearing form was the oldest house I'd seen built of stone—sturdy, thick walls of limestone, cut and chiseled by hand, glued and pieced together with mortar and care. But other than the stubborn-standing walls, the structure was failing, falling apart. A precarious wooden porch hugged the front facade like a climber barely clinging to a cliff. A pair of entry doors dangled on hinges like front teeth waiting for the tooth fairy. And long-ago missing windows left gaping holes in a house that no longer smiled.

Yet despite its deterioration, I *loved* that old house. Expressing compassion for the abandoned structure, I snapped photos and painted pictures of it to document its heartache. I visited it on a regular basis as if catching up with a longlost relative. And in one way true kinship existed.

This first old house to haunt me with a passion for architecture was no longer owned by family, but it *had* been built by my great-great-grandfather. After serving as a Texas Ranger and later as a member of the Texas Calvary during the Civil War, he married and eventually built a permanent dwelling. Grandpa Gholson spent two years assisting a stonemason in quarrying, hauling, squaring, and laying the stone for a house that I would later come to love.

Whenever I can, I return to visit the current owners of this old family homestead; the place holds my hand like a friend. Looking back now, I know how Grandpa and Grandma Gholson's sturdy stone house influenced my eventual interest in historic preservation. The headstrong walls of their former home instilled in me an appreciation for that which holds age and is crafted by *hand*. My ancestors gifted me with a love for old buildings and never knew it.

In architecture school, my infatuation with Italy also blossomed with one special structure, the Palladian villa I've mentioned several times—the Villa Rotonda in Vicenza. Like my great-great-grandfather's house, this structure was symbolic of a world I would later explore in greater depth. Both were inspirational icons. The stone house in Texas opened the door to architecture—and Palladio's villa first drew me to Italy.

In particular, artists, architects, and writers have been going to Italy for centuries, as much to discover themselves as to partake of the Italian experience: witness the remnants of antiquity, admire great masterpieces of art and architecture, savor the special quality of life—*la dolce vita*.

My quest is no different. I seek Italy to find myself as much as to uncover a country and its people. Seeking Italy inflates my soul!

Collect Postcards and Slides

Among other things, I collect postcards and slides of Italy—new and secondhand *cartoline postale* and diminutive square frames of mysterious content. I solicit friends who are about to depart to send postcards stamped Assisi, Viaréggio, or Montepulciano. And upon their return, I beg them to show me their slides.

"You mean you *really* want to see our vacation slides?"

"Oh, *yes*," I respond. "But can we start with the ones you took in Italy?" I make sure David and I don't get stuck watching *colorless* English gardens or *boring* nude beaches on the French Riviera!

"Just Italy you say? We don't have very many—maybe five hundred slides of Rome, Siena, and Florence, plus three or four slide trays covering side trips. *Oh*, and there's Venice! All together it'll take a couple of hours or more—are you sure?"

"*Yes*, absolutely. It'll be great!" I reply, reinforcing the position that watching someone else's vacation slides will be a genuine treat for David and me. But I don't go overboard. I don't reveal my true thoughts. I never mention that a slide show seems like a Mt. Vesuvius eruption compared to our typical Saturday night entertainment—staying at home.

I confess. People who shoot slides but never photos are not normal. Slide connoisseurs are a special breed—not your ordinary snapshooters. We thrive on an element of mystery, on minuscule imagery that doesn't reveal its secrets until projected and focused on a screen.

Why look at something as easy as photographs when you can have *slides*? Why miss the opportunity to hold framed snippets to the light for a hint of recognition, like looking at paint chips the size of postage stamps and visualizing a new color for your walls? Why collect something if it can't be magnified on a super screen the size of a barn?

Then there's the economics. Film and developing costs are often less per image for slides than for photos. For major trips, I calculate the numbers (jiggle them if necessary) and explain them to a skeptical husband. So what if you *also* need an archival cabinet for storage, a light box for previewing, a Kodak Carousel projector with auto-focus and a slide advancement system, ten dozen slide trays (for images you're not ready to store), two projection screens (one permanent and one portable), a hundred-foot extension cord, and replacement bulbs (special projector lamps the price of a house payment). And then there's popcorn and soft drinks, smelling salts for those you put to sleep, and a pointer. Every presenter needs a pointer, either one with a beam of light (perfect for spotlighting snoozers), or the old-fashioned extendible kind that looks like a pocket pen for nerds. My favorite!

One reason David hates to travel with me is that I carry a ton of camera equipment and film that I don't want zapped by gorilla x-ray at the airport. After surviving the ticket-counter line to check his luggage, David is eager as a race-horse to go to the departure gate without further delay. So of course he's deliriously happy when I back up the security checkpoint like fans queuing to buy tickets for the Rolling Stones.

What can I say? I'm a skeptic. I don't trust the posted signs at airports—notices telling me my film won't be damaged by x-ray equipment. No one can convince me it's *good* to be smacked with megadoses of radiation that turn bones inside out like a skeleton.

For our departure to Italy, David was ready to turn around and go home as soon as we arrived at the airport. His *fondness* for travel exposed itself right away: "Why do you always have to drag that stuff out and make a scene? They're going to zap it anyway, so I don't know why you bother every time we go some place."

"If I don't *show* them the cameras and lenses to prove that they're real, they'll scatter my ratty underwear all over the conveyer belt. I don't mind the x-ray when there's no film in the cameras. But do *you* want to repack my bag after they figure out what I've got?"

Hoping to avoid at least one exposure (since the effect of x-rays on film is cumulative), I engage Sunday manners that would make my mother-in-law proud. Gently, I relinquish my Ziplock baggies full of film for hand inspection. At the same time, however, I notice that David's happy-traveler status is undergoing further compromise. He's patting one foot and eyeballing my film as it's scrutinized, one roll at a time—three dozen rolls of slide film, previously reduced in bulk since I've stripped its store-bought packaging. Opening each canister is easy, but slow.

Meanwhile, I'm performing before an audience that is restless. I hear drums start to beat. With an accomplice status of a driver during a bank robbery, I notice my partner slipping away, unnoticed. He's mixing with the crowd that is staring at me, the enemy—the bad guy, the primary suspect stealing their time.

And then without a nod or other sign of intention, David sneaks on ahead, in pretense of traveling solo. But am I bitter? Not at all. Instead, I'm thankful. Just as easily, he could have lingered with the natives to give me a hard time: "Hey, lady. What's the problem? I got a plane to catch!"

After the first dozen rolls of film, I apparently receive a nuisance rating that is off the meter and am waved on without further delay. My film, precious to me as gold that will tarnish, has avoided zap-city thus far! Thanking the official for sparing my treasure, I handle my film like eggs—thirty-six parcels of golden eggs, to be returned to their carefully packed nest.

Slide lovers carry triple the film of ordinary snapshooting tourists—a minimum of two thirty-six-exposure rolls per day, or more for major sites. We justify the expense of our habit by repeating cozy quips: "It's better to take too many slides than not enough" (whatever that means) and "Film is cheaper than time." We're fortune cookies outfitted with cameras, pretending to be witty with our sayings, trying to divert attention by asking, "Is *anything* more precious than time?"

Several categories of slideshooters exist. Some photographers take slides of monuments and buildings to the exclusion of human beings, momentarily denying the existence of man, woman, and child (my own modus operandi). Other vacationers snap great panoramic views capturing everything in sight while ignoring all detail. Still others are fond of bird's-eye views. They climb to the top of everything and look down onto cities and sites.

And then there are the tourists who are brave enough to *act* like tourists, allowing themselves to shoot I-was-here shots: riding in a gondola, feeding pigeons in Piazza San Marco, or posing with a hand to one side—as they support the Leaning Tower of Pisa.

"Don't you ever take pictures of people?" my mother-in-law once asked.

"No," I had replied, "not if I don't have to!"

Now I plead. What's so terrible about waiting for cathedral grounds to clear—to enter a human-free zone? I like buildings to be the center of attention. If I take shots with people milling around, sitting on steps, or pointing and laughing, my slides will be quickly outdated and the subject matter distorted or forgotten. "Oh man, would you look at those hiphugger bellbottoms! When did you take these slides?" Instead of cooing about the craftsmanship of carved stonework or diapered brickwork, slide viewers will comment on hairstyles and fashions. ("Can you believe the size of that hair . . ., the height of those heels . . ., the length of that skirt?")

I want my architecture, my historical buildings, to be frozen in time—slide images that require an architect to notice whether a building is pre- or post-restoration because one critical piece of the architectural puzzle is either missing or intact.

I want slides telling subtle stories.

"That middle bay of stonework appears to be infill. It's obvious they didn't use material from the original quarry, for the color's not right. And the tool marks are crude. It doesn't match the quality of the earlier work."

Or, "Looks like they've replaced the windows at the top of that building—not enough lites (glass panes) in the sashes. Two over two is all wrong for the period."

For the most part, my husband is tolerant of my position, enlightened about my stance on shooting slides without people. He even appreciates the merits of my point of view. But David's patience *is* slightly pushed to the limit in two situations when I'm trying to shoot slides: 1) when he's waiting on me waiting for a building site to *empty*, and 2) when he's watching me wait for the sun to appear from behind clouds at the precise moment all the people go *inside*. Without fail there's a straggler—a lagging tourist who insists on reading every sign, absorbing every detail, or who drags a last-minute cigarette (daring to smoke on my time!). The moment of opportunity is first painfully elusive, then flashingly brief—that skinny split-second when a photographer's world aligns and the shutter can click.

So far, I've resorted to most everything. I've told rub-
bernecking gawkers that the grass is too wet to walk on.
I've suggested to amateur photographers that the light is
better in the afternoon. I've lied that the later tour is worth
coming back for. And for my next trip I've printed a
"Grounds Closed" sign to carry and post as needed!

Photographers seeking slides with unconventional
views also dare to be oddballs in public: assume unnatur-
al positions, wear eccentric garb, and talk gibberish to
inanimate objects. David was alarmed and embarrassed
the first time I bellied up to a gutter downpipe for a detail
of a dolphin leader head (an ornament at the top of a
downspout) that had fallen on the ground. He was curious the first time I spread-eagled myself over the hood of
a Volkswagen Beetle to get the best angle on a Victorian
in San Francisco, when someone had parked their car in
my way. And he vacated the premises once in
Philadelphia when I focused too closely on the private
parts of a figural sculpture and started babbling to
myself. But mostly, like the time I asked to sit on his
shoulders for a better view of The Breakers mansion in
Newport, he ignores me.

And other odd habits? Out of affection or pity, I'm
known by my husband as a woman who wears "round-
toed" shoes. So it's probably inconsequential when I also
don fashionable photographers' attire (bulking up like a
wrestler in a multi-pocketed vest) and shriek about sites

while David is driving. "Look, look! Did you see that? Did you see what we passed?"

After braking and shouting sweet comments at me for scaring him half to death, David is oddly irritated to discover he almost jackknifed the car for a dilapidated old building, not an unexpected car. You'd think he'd be *pleased* it was only a house—with arched eyebrow windows, peaking through shingles you can't buy anymore!

Exploring my passion for Italy through postcards is another hobby of mine. The first time I came home from Italy with a pouch full of *blank* cards, I recognized a potential huge problem. Trip after trip after trip, what was I to do with my postcards? Should I cram them in a shoebox and stuff them under the bed—out of sight, out of mind? Or display and call them a *collection*, as if giving them a name would justify the action of buying too many?

Clearly, accumulating too many postcards is detrimental to the concept of traveling light. So I've learned to be more prudent. I no longer buy postcards from cities and towns where I've already been! Admittedly, it's not a high standard, considering that new-to-me places in Italy greatly outnumber the places I've come to know. But it's a start.

One of the best strategies for adding to my postcard collection is simple, discovered by accident. I send favorite cards to friends and relatives in Texas, and, like tossing old bubble gum from a fast-moving car, my postcards come back to me. (Am I the only person who saves everything?) Most people hand them over without my asking, or often after cleaning out a drawer. Either way, it's convenient. I get to add meaningful items to my collection, without breaking my back to tote them home. One card at a time, the weight of paper goods adds up in a hurry!

Why postcards fascinate is easy to understand. They extend simple handshakes from thousands of miles away. Mailing a postcard, with a few dashed lines, is like sending a tiny piece of myself. I love to browse sidewalk displays for special images I think my grandmother will like: "I tossed a coin in this fountain and made a wish for you today." I find eye-catching city or street scenes to send to my mother and in-laws: "I'm sitting at a tiny table in Arezzo, licking a mountain of gelato as I write!" For David (or to send to myself), I choose postcards of historic land-marks: "The carved marble you see here is incredibly handsome up close. Can *we* come back to visit this build-ing some day?"

Collecting postcard ephemera is a fun fling with Italy for me, a paper *festa* of curiosities. The cards are small, fairly uniform in size, easy to organize, and cheap. I store mine in clear plastic containers with hinged lids, instead of in albums—clear boxes about an inch and a half deep, slightly larger than the postcards themselves. I stand the boxes on edge to display the top image, and periodically, I shuffle the cards in each box so that new ones get rotated to the top.

And fingerprints? Archival protective sleeves, specifically sized for postcards, are the ideal solution. I like the polyester mylar type with a "fold-lock" design. They may cost more than the sandwich-bag-looking ones, but they make my cheap postcards look grand.

Less clumsy than albums, small boxes make it easy to carry a postcard collection to restaurants. A boxed assortment allows David and me to ponder our anniversary journeys while dining out—pasta or pizza without doubt.

We also rummage through old *cartoline postale* and read aloud the travel experiences of strangers: "Here we are in beautiful Venice, it surely is something. Yesterday morning we visited 9 churches. This afternoon we fed the pigeons at St. Mark's square . . ."—May 2, 1904. Another postcard (dated 1909 and addressed to a Ruth in Omaha, Nebraska) has a canal scene and a penciled message on the front: "Is not this an ideal place to go boat riding?" It rivals the originality of a few postcard lines of my own, but I love it! The date could be 1909 or 1999—words from Venice need never change.

I'm also snared by the tattered *francobolli*, the old stamps still stuck on my vintage collectibles. Frozen in time by their denomination, the stamps intrigue me, and cause me to ponder the people who sent the cards long ago. Did these travelers love Italy the way I love Italy? Were they passionate and Italy-crazed upon studying Baedeker guidebooks and dreamy-eyed after seeing drawings and paintings by Turner, Ruskin, or Sargent? Or, perhaps, were they simply captivated by the spectacle of travel after reading the romantic words of Henry James? Or Edith Wharton?

Relish the Ritual of the Passeggiata

om Snyder convinced my husband to go to Italy. It's true that I connived, enticed, and bribed my spouse with glowing prospects of riding a bicycle in Tuscany. Yes, the trip was to be our twentieth anniversary celebration. But honestly, I believe it was the former *Late, Late Show* host, Tom Snyder, that finally made the difference.

A few years ago, David came across an old news story he'd clipped and saved from 1995. Picked up from *The Palm Beach Post*, the piece was presented in our local paper: "Snyder Experiences Renaissance," with the caption, "Talk show host Tom Snyder says a recent trip to Italy has calmed him and changed his life." Reading about

Snyder's life-altering experiences of flying through a lightning storm and traveling in Italy, David was awed by the celebrity's praise of three huge priorities among Italians—family, lifestyle, and the Catholic Church. According to the talk show host, a customer with a wad of cash for a watch at Gucci's in Rome doesn't mean a thing, if it's one o'clock in the afternoon and time to shut down for food and a siesta. Oblivious to deal-making, life outweighs *lire* in Italy.

My husband, who gobbles his workday burger in three bites, spitting politics between well-timed gulps, was notably impressed. For years I'd admired the *Late, Late Show* host, but my devotion rose exponentially after seeing David's reaction to Snyder's "Italian experience." Anyone who can pump my husband with thoughts of foreign travel deserves recognition. He who loves Italy the way I love Italy deserves flag-waving thanks from me. *Mille grazie*, Tom Snyder!

Once in Italy, it took David only a few days to embrace the softened lifestyle and to add a fourth item to Snyder's all-important list. Football. Italians passionately pursue *il cacio*—the kick! Or, soccer, as it's called in the United States. True fans will find it necessary to read Joe McGinniss' book called *The Miracle of Castel di Sangro*. From victories to scandal, no detail escapes McGinniss as he chronicles a year in the lives of individuals associated with a small-town soccer team in the Abruzzo region of Italy.

A Sunday bicycle ride, one afternoon in Vicenza, confirmed the Italian love of soccer for David and me. On the way to the train station to return our cruiser-style rentals, David and I repeatedly found our route circumvented by traffic, closed roads, and guarded barricades. When, out of nowhere, without explanation to me whatsoever, David suddenly darted toward an arm-swinging policeman in the middle of an intersection—as if flushing a covey of quail.

Holding my breath in horror as my husband prodded some form of communication, I conjured ugly visions of being carted off to jail—either for butchering the Italian language prior to a soccer match, or for being taken as complaining, not curious, Americans. Brag-hardy tourists from Texas, no less. Made obvious by David's first word: "BARN-jarno!"

Fortunately for us, an English-speaking officer (a miracle of gargantuan proportion) unzipped a quick smile and informed us that all roads were blocked from the station to the stadium until Naples fans could be *escorted* to the game on foot. But for now, as if returning a favor for a buddy, the Texas-friendly guard halted traffic for us with his upheld hands and a whistle—getting us closer to the train station and the big event!

Responding to our thanks, however, he quickly turned somber again, offering no more than a faint chuckle and final comment: "Prego. Prego. But please pray for me that nothing happens today. I wish to return home safely to my family tonight."

David and I looked at each other. "He's serious!" I said. "Genuinely worried about the possibility of a riot."

Glancing back, we witnessed our seconds-ago smiling policeman dispensing nasty disapproval with "talking" hands and brutal Italian phrases—aimed at the driver of a Fiat who had dared to pass on our heels. How easy it was to believe that the verbal attack might well have been directed at us!

Everyone in town was headed for the afternoon confrontation with Naples, a major rival. Emotions on the field and in the stands ran equally high. Later, we heard that one fan had been killed the previous year during another Naples-Vicenza battle.

"Why don't we ride closer to see what's going on?" I said, unable to choke curiosity. "We're so close not to go. It'll be easy on bicycles, don't you think?"

"They'll be in riot gear, you know—the police," David remarked, curious like me. "But it'll be fun to tell your brother about the wild fans *and* the armed guards."

So, in the middle of a human stream flowing to the stadium, we too were sucked in by the current, the energy, the passion—bodies pulled by the magnetic force of imminent conflict. As we pedaled closer, our hearts beat faster amid a mounting chorus: "Allez Vicenza! Allez Vicenza!"

At two guarded entrances, we sneaked peeks across the soccer field at a confetti-looking crowd on the opposite side of a bare-bones concrete arena. After observing with amusement several fans trying to "talk their way in," we headed for the main entrance to witness the enemy procession—Naples spectators soon due from the train station. Stopping at a cautious distance, I removed my lens cover in anticipation of recording the action.

Mistaking the arrival of the southern fans was impossible. The dim roar from the Vicentines quickly climaxed to a serious rumble as armed troops marched before us in convoy, displaying head-to-toe battle garb like a modern Roman army—helmets, flak jackets, body shields, and submachine guns. Their dark blue uniforms with white leather belts and matching holsters appeared to be *carabinieri* attire (famously designed by Giorgio Armani), while their clear protective shields (large enough to squat behind) were boldly branded *POLIZIA*. Barely visible through a wall of armor, the Neapolitan caravan quickly disappeared inside, swallowed by a mouth of gray concrete.

Lazy and lingering, watching the disbandment, David and I finally rose to attention when one officer started walking straight toward us to deposit his swinging submachine gun in the back of a nearby van. This was my chance—my opportunity to shoot slides, scrutinize his regalia in detail! Then I changed my mind.

Feeling simultaneously stupid and terrified, I quickly dropped my camera to my side, out of sight. In a rebound of sanity, I'd suddenly decided it was risky to point anything at a Beretta-toting *carabinieri* guard.

While the stadium thrashed and screamed to contain its skirmish, we proceeded at last to the train station to return our rented cruisers. David, waiting to get his driver's license back from deposit, was excited to hear a radio blasting the game and asked about the score. One of the rental clerks, interpreting the Texan twang with ease (or simply answering the only question that could possibly be important at the moment), responded in a serious tone, "Uno, uno."

David next took a chance on impressing them. "Allez Vicenza! Allez Vicenza!" he said.

"Allez Vicenza! Allez Vicenza!" both clerks fired back in rapid response. "Grazie, grazie. Allez Vicenza!" David's enthusiastic support was overwhelmingly received and he gloated.

Later that evening, dining at an outdoor pizzeria close to our hotel, David asked our young waiter about the outcome of the sporting event.

"Uno, uno," said the waiter, with a hint of sadness. I guess no team accepts a standoff with joy. But was there more?

Never one to pass on a good opportunity, my husband again decided he'd try to charm the locals. Declaring allegiance when his pizza arrived, he proudly repeated his earlier cheer: "Allez Vicenza! Allez Vicenza!"

But this time it backfired. Instead of "Allez Vicenza!" in return, the waiter frowned and said, "No. Allez Napoli! Allez Napoli!"

Our waiter was a southern *import*?

Without missing a beat, our attendant then turned and pointed to all the other servers in sight, who joined him in chorus with "Allez Napoli! Allez Napoli!" Snickers rippled and echoed along the walkways and around the corner to the *piazza* for all ears to partake of the blunder. Unfortunately for David, the *entire* wait staff was proudly Neapolitan.

First pretending to be invisible, David finally grinned and said, "I sure hope they don't spit on *your* food." Unlike my pasta order, his *prosciutto* and *funghi* pizza had arrived long ago!

Italy is so much more complex than can be defined in terms of simple pleasures. Yet one of her customs is a simple, daily routine that I fondly embrace. It's the gentle art of the *passeggiata*—the leisurely Italian stroll at evening time, up and down city streets, around and across crowded *piazze*.

For me, the pleasure of the promenade is heightened by stretching the event into stages. On round one I congratulate myself for walking off extra calories. (What a marvelous thing I'm doing!) During the next half hour, I reply to a fast-fading willpower by focusing on something *other* than ice cream. (That's a lovely gray suit in the window!) By the third time around the *piazza*, however, I simply give in. I surrender and point to a final sinful flavor for the day. It *is* my last chance, after all!

"Take your soul for a stroll," writes Phil Cousineau in *The Art of Pilgrimage: The Seeker's Guide to Making Travel Sacred*. In Texas we call it "cruising," and we do it in a car. Otherwise, it's the same.

David and I grew up in a small rural town. And our Texas teenage version of the *passeggiata* was driving a car (or pickup) up and down Main Street, circling and pausing on the square, communicating to others through open windows. We drove to the beat of the music blasting from our eight-track tapes, sounding cool, looking cool—or so we hoped.

Like Italians strolling arm in arm discussing love affairs, politics, and soccer, we cruised and talked of girl-friends, boyfriends, and Friday night football. Instead of linking elbows Italian-style, we drove with our elbows sticking out windows in casual pose, while signaling subtle greetings to passing friends—one finger gently lifted from a steering wheel.

For now, a little of Italy has rubbed off on me. I drive less and walk more. An Italian rustic bread at a neighborhood bakery entices me to march for my loaf. And like Venetians marking distances by bridge count, I walk the *one* steep hill to and from a video store, sauntering downhill, struggling uphill, but ever so proud when I make the effort.

I praise Italy for slowing me down, renewing my spirit. Whenever I'm rushed in Austin to do this or that, I now ask myself simple questions: If I were in Todi, would I be madly racing across town for the perfect gift? If I were in Orvieto, would I be wolfing down a sandwich—instead of *idly* savoring each bite, cherishing a gentle moment for myself?

It is the *land* of Italy that makes me breathe deeply, taking it all in—the sandy starkness of freshly plowed fields, the orderliness of olive trees and grapevines balancing nature and man. The deep furrows and dirt clots of Tuscany's landscape remind me of tilled acreage from my childhood—fields in Central Texas where my father plowed at night when he thought it might rain (though it seldom did). These were the fields where my brothers and I picked up pieces of flint and limestone to clear the land when we were young. Each season's cultivation unearthed new crusty fragments for us to collect and pile along the fence lines, or deposit in washed-out gullies.

I wonder about the rocks from the fields in Tuscany. Have they all been gathered for so many centuries that plowings no longer expose new ones? Have all the discarded pebbles and boulders been used to shape the compounds I see on distant hills—used as rubble in thick stone walls and layered deep behind coats of stucco?

Or fences. Were the rocks used to build solid enclosures, or retaining walls that hold terraced gardens?

We never built anything with the stone from our land when I was a child. Though fallen rock fences were familiar to me. They existed as faded boundaries, evidence of intensive labor from long ago. I remember those crumbling walls and their connection to the earth where I stood. Each rock had been carefully selected, skillfully placed in its position—an indigenous piece of a puzzle from the past.

But I do recall one special fence my father and brothers built that was *of* the land. Much like the pioneer rock fences, its construction required patience. While most fences were quickly strung with barbed or netted wire, this one was made of lashed cedar staves, side by side on end, like vertical log walls of a territorial fort. Associating the slender posts with the cedar saplings on our mountain, I was fascinated by the fence's slow progression. Each stave was selected to crook in unison with its neighbor, joined at the hip and partnered for life. In its own way, the cedar fence was instructive—early schooling that the best things in life take more time.

Learning how nature embroiders timelessness into our built world is a lesson that is evident in Italy: cut stones for a dimpled walkway instead of a poured concrete path, a vine-covered pergola offering perennial, dappled shade instead of a hard-edged shelter ignoring a warm winter sun.

Italy's landscape keeps me feverish, renews my spirit, fuels me toward new beginnings. Distant, yet similar in certain ways to what I grew up with, it binds me to home. Gentle, serene, open, secure. Farmed land makes sense to me. Its purpose is honest—visibly noted by seasons.

Every morning I wake to thoughts of Italy. I wonder how the weather is yawning in Siena or Vicenza as I glance out to see what's happening in Texas. As I canvass the yard for morning newspapers, I picture Veronese locals standing for their breakfast at a local bar. As I pour a bowl of high-fiber cereal and rice milk, I recall the sloping vineyards and hillside gardens where I hiked along the Cinque Terra.

While a love affair with Italy must ultimately be consummated on foreign soil, the courtship (without or before leaving home) is a sensual part of the journey. Like climbing hundreds of steps to reach a summit view, indulging in Italy is *dazzling* when you prepare for the pleasure one step at a time.

Each day, each month, each year my fever continues to ebb and flow and I travel to Italy as often as I can—either alone or with friends. But I'm longing, waiting, looking forward to the moment when a joint adventure will again surface for my spouse and me. I have no inkling of when the opportunity will come, when we'll resume a tangled romance in Tuscany. But already—in anticipation—I've started hoarding David's old underwear again! I expect I'll always be tossing a few Jockeys in secret on the road, since he's destined to carry too many clean clothes for life. And again, I will *call* our journey a "bicycle tour"—as enticement to my non-traveling husband.

Meanwhile, I dose myself daily with every possible excuse and manner of absorbing a country I love. Like swallowing time-release pills that dispense Italy into my life, I continue to write with an Italian pen on Venetian and Florentine note cards, and roll out fresh pasta while standing in my Italianized *cucina*—with its walls reflecting but a few of the twenty colors of my sunny Italy. Movie soundtracks and opera arias keep flooding my life with music—*Il Postino*, *Life Is Beautiful*, Mario Lanzo, Maria Callas. And I'll forever be *researching* American gelati, expecting postcards from traveling friends, and relishing the ritual of the *passeggiata*.

My passion for Italy keeps me stirring, helps me recognize and follow new paths, helps me discover *la dolce vita*—in Texas: a bicycle ride in the Hill Country, a patch of earth for sprouting a garden, a good book and the *time* to enjoy it. Blessed by an abundance of simple pleasures around me, my reawakened spirit, via Italy, soars!

Nebulous Notes and Web Sites

Here are a few details that readers may enjoy or find useful. Please bear in mind that the "facts" are somewhat nebulous and are not intended to represent any conclusive evaluation of available information. In other words, the details are scattered tidbits but correct at the time of going to press.

Furthermore, I cannot ensure the status, accuracy, or appropriateness of materials accessed via Internet. (Without question, Web site URL's may change or disappear altogether.)

1. UPDATE PASSPORTS AND LUGGAGE

Passport and other helpful travel information is available from the U. S. State Department's Web site (http://travel.state.gov).

Two travel supply sources, Magellan's® (http://www.magellans.com) and TravelSmith® (http://www.travelsmith.com) offer nice selections of luggage, clothing, and travel accessories, with easy-to-use Web sites. I'm also spoiled by a local travel store in Austin, TravelFest™ by Pace (http://www.travelfest.com).

Need help packing? The Fair Air Coalition sponsors a helpful Web site (http://www.flyana.com/pack.html) with hints on travel and packing.

See Chapter 11 notes for information on Tommasini bicycles.

2. DISPLAY MAPS AS ART

Our Heritage Maps at In Italy™ Online (http://www.initaly.com/ads/maps.htm) and MapQuest Map Store (http://www.mapquest.com) are two online sources for Italian maps. Most major bookstores and numerous independent travel bookstores also carry a good supply. It *is* more fun to handle a map before actually purchasing it!

Italo Calvino's *Invisible Cities* was translated from the Italian by William Weaver (1974). This book is impossible to describe, and perhaps, that's a part of its charm.

Erma Bombeck's column, "Men Never Ask Directions—August 24, 1969," was delightfully discovered by me in her book, *Forever, Erma* (1996).

3. TRAVEL THROUGH MOVIES

Obscure Italian movie rentals are easier to find at off-beat video stores. Instead of searching the large video chains, try the small independents (often located near college campuses).

Several of the general movie-related Web sites are useful for information about current film offerings. Yet other sources provide better specialized listings of Italy-related movies. For accessing movie-related pages at In Italy™ Online (http://www.initaly.com/index.htm), first click "Italy at Your House," then "Arts," then "Movies." Mama's Cucina at the "Ragú" Web site (http://www.ragu.com) also has a nice listing organized by genre and geographical setting; click "Find It" and enter "film festival" in search.

The Venice Biennale (http://www.labiennale.org) or (http://www.biennaleprogram.org) is held in Venice from June to September every odd-numbered year, though the Film Festival occupies the nearby Lido every year in August and/or September.

California's Marin County Italian Film Festival (http://www.italianfilm.com) is held every other fall. In recent years, it has been held at the Marin County Civic Center complex in San Rafael, California.

Elizabeth Barrett Browning's *Casa Guidi Windows* (published separately in 1851) was named after the Brownings' home in Florence. The version I have is included in a paperback volume called *Elizabeth Barrett Browning: Aurora Leigh and Other Poems* (1995). I found "The Englishman in Italy" in an 1898 leather-bound edition I purchased called *Pocket Volume of Selections from The Poetical Works of Robert Browning*.

4. Learn to Speak a Little Italian

Two Web sites for exploring the Italian language are In Italy™ Online

(http://www.initaly.com/ads/language.htm), a language
course (many others exist); and the Ragú site, with its
"Learn to Speak Italian" pages
(http://www.eat.com/learn-italian/index.html). *The
Magazine of La Cucina Italiana's* Web site
(http://www.piacere.com) also contains a nice food
glossary.

The excerpt from Mark Twain's essay, "Italian
Without a Master," is from *The $30,000 Bequest and
Other Stories* (1906). It was also previously published
in *Harper's Weekly* (1904).

5. SAVOR THE FOOD AND DRINK OF REGIONAL ITALY

Information on Slow Food International, also known
as Arcigola (http://www.arcigola.com), was partially
derived from two printed sources: Frommer's *Food
Lover's Companion to Italy* (1996) by Marc and Kim
Millon, and *Eating in Italy* (1998) by Faith Heller
Willinger.

The Hotel Cipriani in Venice makes an *aperitivo*
called a *tintoretto*. It's made with pomegranate juice
and sparkling wine.

The sponsor of The Harry's Bar and American Grill
International Imitation Hemingway Competition is

PEN Center USA West (http://www.pen-usa-west.org), an organization of professional writers that promotes freedom of expression through a variety of literary programs.

Giuliano Hazan teaches Italian cooking classes in the United States and Italy. He is author of *The Classic Pasta Cookbook* (1993) and *Every Night Italian* (2000). Hazan is also developing a new cooking school to be located in a villa near Verona, offering picturesque accommodations for cooking-school students. Also of interest, Giuliano Hazan's mother, Marcella Hazan, is the reigning queen of Italian cooking: *Marcella's Italian Kitchen* (1987), *Essentials of Classic Italian Cooking* (1992), and *Marcella Cucina* (1997). And his father, Victor Hazan, is known for his wine expertise: *Italian Wine* (1982).

My first inkling of the broad offerings by Italian cooking schools operating in Italy came by way of Vancouver, Canada, where Margaret Cowan publishes *Your Guide to 82 Decadent Cooking Holidays in Italy*, complete with updates. Her Web site (http://www.italycookingschools.com) is chock-full of enticing itineraries.

ShawGuides (http://www.shawguides.com) also produces an interesting publication called *The Guide to Cooking Schools: Cooking Schools, Courses, Vacations, Apprenticeships and Wine Instruction Throughout the World*; see "Cooking Schools-Recreational." (My copy is a 1998 edition.)

The television shows listed for Italian-cooking chefs may not be available in all viewing areas, and at least one show currently is not being aired. *Bugialli's Italy* (no specific Web site located) is shown on public television stations, as is *Lidia's Italian Table* (http://www.lidiasitaly.com). *Molto Mario* (http://www.foodtv.com) is a Food Network program that I watch from time to time. *Biba's Italian Kitchen* was discontinued when The Learning Channel dropped all of its cooking shows; see (http://www.biba-restaurant.com). And, my cable company no longer offers (or I'm unwilling to pay extra for!) *Ciao Italia*™ (http://www.ciaoitalia.com) and *CucinaAmore*™ (http://www.cucinaamore.com). Each is a PBS series.

Conde Nast's "Epicurious Food" (http://www.epicurious.com) ia also a special treat: within the Epicurious site, look under "Letter from Italy" for a wonderful archive of Faith Heller Willinger's writings on food and Italy. Lastly, I couldn't resist checking out Italy's 1999 Winery of the Year (http://castellobanfi.com); also (http://www.wine.it).

6. KEEP A NOTEBOOK, JOURNAL, OR "SCRAPBOX"

A few of the leather journals I have were made in Italy for a company called Daisy Arts (http://www.daisyarts.com), located in Venice, California.

In addition to Natalie Goldberg's *Writing Down the Bones* (1996) and Julia Cameron's The Artist's Way (1992), I'm partial to a book by Susan Wittig Albert titled *Writing from Life, Telling Your Soul's Story* (1996). A few years ago, I enjoyed one of Albert's writing classes sponsored by the Austin Writers' League.

Michael J. Gelb's book *How to Think Like Leonardo da Vinci: Seven Steps to Genius Every Day* (1998) is a wonderful hands-on way to enjoy a "piece" of Italy. Gelb has also produced a coordinating notebook.

Over 30,000 Web pages (not sites) for Leonardo da Vinci exist—too many to decipher! On the other hand, the Monticello Web site

(http://www.monticello.org), sponsored by the
Thomas Jefferson Memorial Foundation, Inc., is an
easy destination full of historical data that is
organized in a number of ways. The site also features
an online book and garden store.

See Chapter 12 notes for information on Andrea
Palladio.

I first wrote about our "vertical brick dwelling
becoming a leaning Tower of Pisa" in a magazine article for *Old-House Journal*, "Living a Double Life"
(September/October 1997).

Susan Wooldridge's book *Poemcrazy: Freeing Your
Life with Words* (1996) is invaluable for poetry
lovers. And even if you think you don't like poetry,
her book may very well change your mind.

7. TRAVEL THROUGH BOOKS

The guidebook used for our last-night stay in Milan was
Rick Steves' Italy 1997, an ongoing favorite of mine.

Erica Bauermeister, Jesse Larsen, and Holly Smith co-
edited *500 Great Books by Women: A Reader's Guide*
(1994).

The Diary of an Idle Woman in Italy by Frances Elliot is a small rare book in my personal collection. It is printed with no date, but research reveals that the book was published c. 1871-1872. Elliot also authored additional travel-related books, including one on Sicily and another about Rome.

The Sisters in Crime's™ Web site (http://www.books.com/sinc) will lure you for hours on end. Its author listings are extensive.

Fabulous "book" sites are plentiful. The American Booksellers' Association has a dual Internet presence, (http://www.bookweb.org) and (http://www.book-sense.com), that promotes its members' stores. Readers can go there to find bookstores in their own communities. BookZone (http://www.bookzone.com) is also a good site for locating books produced by small publishers.

In Austin, an independent bookstore called Book People (http://www.bookpeople.com) is naturally a favorite destination of mine—it's within walking distance from my house. But, without doubt, the most exciting bookstore experience in Texas is author Larry McMurtry's "booktown," a small-town bookstore in Archer City (south of Wichita Falls) called Booked Up—building after building of new, used, and rare books. The phone number is (940) 574-2511.

Although most bookstores also stock books on tape, a few sources specifically offer audio books for sale and/or rent. Several offer rental transactions by mail, a super solution for book lovers who live in remote locations and must drive significant distances for shopping! Typically, these businesses have a healthy selection of abridged and unabridged recordings in their inventories; search travel, fiction, ect. I recently checked out NewStar Media's Web site called Audio Universe.Com (http://www.audiouniverse.com). It features sound samples and in the future will have download capabilities.

You may also find these Italy-related magazines of interest: *Italian Food, Wine and Travel* (1-888-656-6669), *Italy Italy* (http://www.italyitalymagazine.com), *Italia Magazine* (http://www.italiamag.com), *The Magazine of La Cucina Italiana* (http://www.piacere.com), *La Dolce Vita Magazine* (http://www.ladolcevitamag.com).

8. INDULGE IN MILANESE FASHION (OR PLANT A GARDEN)

Fashion-related Web sites are abundant, yet I include but two for easy reference: Made-In-Italy-On-Line

(http://www.made-in-italy.com) and DolceVita™
(http://www.dolcevita.com).

A specialty garden store in central Austin called
Gardens (http://www.gardens.citysearch.com) is where
I've purchased Italian seed varieties and terra cotta
pots imported from Italy.

The recipe I used for frying zucchini blossoms (and
sage leaves) was taken from Carol Field's cookbook
*In Nonna's Kitchen: Recipes and Traditions from
Italy's Grandmothers* (1997), page 58, Salvia Fritta.

For general reference, my favorite guidebook to
Italian gardens is *The Garden Lover's Guide to Italy*
(1998), by Penelope Hobhouse. The photographs and
artistic layout of the book will make you drool.

9. EXPERIENCE ITALIAN MUSIC AND OPERA

Mary Chapin Carpenter's song "What If We Went to
Italy," is from her CD titled *A Place in the World* (1996).

The musical aria, with Figaro's catchy self-endorse-
ment from *The Barber of Seville*, is Rossini's "Largo
al factotum."

The male vocalist I mention in regard to the *Rigoletto*
performance in Austin (the one originally from

Abilene, Texas) is Neil Wilson, who now lives in Berlin, Germany.

Michael Barnes, music and theater critic for the *Austin American Statesman* wrote the amazing article I read that was stuffed with *Tosca* trivia: "Forty Days. Forty Nights. Being an Opera Stalker is a Full-Time Job," March 4, 1999.

Music and Performers: Italian Sinfonia (http://www.geocities.com/~italianmusic); Luciano Pavarotti (http://www.lucianopavarotti.it); and Andrea Bocelli (http://www.bocelli.it).

Opera Sites: Opera Web (http://www.opera.it); The Austin Lyric Opera (http://www.austinlyricopera.org); La Fenice in Venice (reliable information unavailable); The Metropolitan Opera in New York City (http://www.metopera.org); and Teatro Olimpico in Vicenza (http://www.olimpico.vicenza.it).

10. CELEBRATE WITH GELATO AND ESPRESSO

Elizabeth David's book, *Harvest of the Cold Months: The Social History of Ice and Ices* was published in 1995 and edited by Jill Norman.

My chosen *gelateria* in Lucca is located on the Piazza

Napoleone and is called *Il Pinguino* (The Penguin). Be sure to ask for the *pinolata* flavor because it's not always labeled. I think they must save it for the locals!

The June 1999 issue of *The Magazine of La Cucina* included a tasty article about ice cream, an instructional guide for making gelato and a review of ice-cream machines; see the Cooking School on page 94.

11. RIDE A BICYCLE AT HOME AND ON TOUR

The exerpt from Edith Wharton's *Italian Backgrounds* was first printed by Scribner in 1905 and reprinted by The Echo Press in 1989.

The Web site for the Giro d'Italia (http://www.giro.energy.it) provides good information for tracking this all-important race in Italy.

In case you want to contemplate something flashy before searching for a new bicycle (http://www.cycling.it), you can explore sexy sites for Italian scooters (http://www.piaggio.com), motorcycles (http://www.ducati.com), and the ubiquitous Italian sports car, Ferrari (http://www.ferrari.com).

The Tommasini bicycle factory
(http://www.tommasini.com) is located in Grosseto,
southwest of Siena in Tuscany.

12. Contemplate the Art and Architecture of Italy

Andrea Palladio's architectural career in the Veneto
region spanned the mid-sixteenth century. His famous
Four Books of Architecture (originally called *I
Quattro Libri dell' Architettura*) was published in
1570, and the first complete English translation was
in 1715. Favorite Palladio-related Web sites include:
http://www.ashmm.com/cultura/palladio
http://www.boglewood.com/palladio/home.html

For exploring virtual museum tours ahead of time, try
these sites: In Italy™ Online
(http://www.initaly.com/index.htm), select "Italy at
Your House"; also Harcourt Brace (http://www.har-
brace.com/art/gardner/RenBar.html); and
(http://www.artchive.com) for Mark Harden's Artchive.

13. Collect Postcards and Slides

Light Impressions
(http://www.lightimpressionsdirect.com) is an archival

supply company with an easy-to-use catalog. In addition to protective (PVC-free) polyester sleeves and polyethylene bags for postcards, they also carry archival boxes, storage solutions for slides, and hundreds of other conservation materials for the serious collector.

14. RELISH THE RITUAL OF THE *PASSEGGIATA*

Unfortunately, Tom Snyder no longer hosts NBC's *Late, Late Show*. The news article that David read about Snyder was in the Show World supplement to the *Austin American Statesman*: "Snyder Experiences Renaissance," August 27, 1995. The original article, written by Paul Lomartire, was reprinted from *The Palm Beach Post*.

Here are two good Web sites for following Italian football (soccer): http://www.soccer.com http://www.justwright.com/rss/links.html

Movies That Depict Italy

This roster of "Italy" movies is first separated by language, then organized by geographical location in chronological order. The boxes are included as a checklist: check once for movies that interest you, twice for movies you've seen.

SELECTIONS WITH ENGLISH SUBTITLES

Calabria; also Rome
❏ ❏ *Flight of the Innocent* (1993)

Campania, Naples
❏ ❏ *The Gold of Naples (1955)*
❏ ❏ *Marriage Italian Style (1964)*

Campania, Lucania
  ❏ ❏ *Christ Stopped at Eboli (1980)*

Campania, Naples and Corzano
  ❏ ❏ *Ciao, Professore!* (1994)

Emilia-Romagna, near Bologna
  ❏ ❏ *The Story of Boys and Girls* (1991)

Latium, Rome
  ❏ ❏ *Open City* (1945)
  ❏ ❏ *The Bicycle Thief* (1948)
  ❏ ❏ *Umberto D.* (1955)
  ❏ ❏ *La Dolce Vita* (1960)

Latium, Rome and region
  ❏ ❏ *Two Women* (1961)

Sicily
  ❏ ❏ *Divorce Italian Style* (1962)
  ❏ ❏ *The Leopard* (1963)

Sicily, Giancaldo
  ❏ ❏ *Cinema Paradiso* (1988)

Sicily, Palermo; also Rome
  ❏ ❏ *Johnny Stecchino* (1992)

Sicily, Isola Salina (north of Sicily)
  ❏ ❏ *Il Postino* (1994) (Dubbed English version
      also available)

Veneto, Venice and Verona
- ❏ ❏ *Senso* (1954)

Veneto, the Lido
- ❏ ❏ *Death in Venice* (1971)

Unidentified or General
- ❏ ❏ *La Strada* (1954)
- ❏ ❏ *The Secret of Santa Vittoria* (1969)
- ❏ ❏ *Farinelli* (1994)

ENGLISH LANGUAGE SELECTIONS

Campania, Naples
- ❏ ❏ *The Great Caruso* (1951)

Campania, Naples and Capri
- ❏ ❏ *It Started in Naples* (1960)

Campania, Naples; also Milan and Rome
- ❏ ❏ *Yesterday, Today, and Tomorrow* (1964) (Dubbed in English)

Campania, Positano; also Venice and Rome
- ❏ ❏ *Only You* (1994)

Latium, Rome
- ❏ ❏ *Quo Vadis* (1951)
- ❏ ❏ *Roman Holiday* (1953)
- ❏ ❏ *Three Coins in the Fountain* (1954)

Latium, Rome (continued)
- ❏ ❏ *The Seven Hills of Rome* (1958)
- ❏ ❏ *The Roman Spring of Mrs. Stone* (1961)
- ❏ ❏ *Rome Adventure* (1962)
- ❏ ❏ *The Belly of an Architect* (1991)

Latium, Sermoneta
- ❏ ❏ *For Roseanna* (1997)

Liguria, the Italian Riviera
- ❏ ❏ *Come September* (1961)

Liguria, Portofino
- ❏ ❏ *Enchanted April* (1992)

Lombardy, Como
- ❏ ❏ *A Month by the Lake* (1995)

Tuscany, Pienza; also Gubbio and Tuscania
- ❏ ❏ *Romeo and Juliet* (1968)

Tuscany, Florence
- ❏ ❏ *A Room with a View* (1986)

Tuscany; also Rome
- ❏ ❏ *A Man in Love* (1987)

Tuscany
- ❏ ❏ *Where Angels Fear to Tread* (1991)

Tuscany, near Lamole
- ❏ ❏ *Much Ado About Nothing* (1993)

Tuscany, near Pienza; also the Lido
  ❏ ❏ *The English Patient* (1996)

Tuscany, heart of Chianti country
  ❏ ❏ *Stealing Beauty* (1996)

Tuscany, Arezzo; and studios in Terni
  ❏ ❏ *Life Is Beautiful* (1998)

Tuscany, Florence
  ❏ ❏ *Tea with Mussolini* (1999)

Tuscany, Montepulciano; also Tivoli and Caparolla
  ❏ ❏ *A Midsummer Night's Dream* (1999)

Umbria, Todi
  ❏ ❏ *The Agony and the Ecstacy* (1965)

Umbria, Assisi
  ❏ ❏ *Brother Son, Sister Moon* (1973)

Veneto, Venice
  ❏ ❏ *Summertime* (1955)
  ❏ ❏ *Don't Look Now* (1973)
  ❏ ❏ *The Merchant of Venice* (1973)
  ❏ ❏ *Dangerous Beauty* (1997)
  ❏ ❏ *The Wings of the Dove* (1997)

Veneto, Verona, Venice; also France
  ❏ ❏ *A Little Romance* (1979)

Unidentified or Miscellaneous
- ❑ ❑ *Von Ryan's Express* (1965)

United States and Sicily
- ❑ ❑ *The Godfather* (1972)
- ❑ ❑ *The Godfather, Part 2* (1974)
- ❑ ❑ *The Godfather, Part 3* (1990)

United States
- ❑ ❑ *The Barretts of Wimpole Street* (1934)
- ❑ ❑ *Moonstruck* (1987)
- ❑ ❑ *Big Night* (1995)

Books That Depict Italy

This roster of "Italy" books generally excludes poetry and reference materials per se, such as travel or cultural arts guidebooks, typical cookbooks, and in-depth biographies or other research. Furthermore, the list reflects titles that interest me, and, as such, is therefore not intended as a conclusive survey. The boxes are included as a checklist: check once for books that interest you, twice for books you've read.

ANTHOLOGIES

Susan **Cahill**, ed.
❏ ❏   *Desiring Italy*, 1997.

Anne **Calcagno**, ed.
❏ ❏ *Travelers' Tales Guides Italy: True Stories of Life on the Road*, 1998.

A. Kenneth **Ciongoli**, and Jay Parini, eds.
❏ ❏ *Beyond the Godfather: Italian American Writers on the Italian American Experience*, 1997.

Alice Leccese **Powers**, ed.
❏ ❏ *Italy in Mind*, 1997.

MEMOIRS AND JOURNALS

Kinta **Beevor**
❏ ❏ *A Tuscan Childhood*, 1993.

Harold **Brodkey**
❏ ❏ *My Venice*, 1998.

Joseph **Brodsky**
❏ ❏ *Watermark*, 1992.

Eleanor **Clark**
❏ ❏ *Rome and a Villa*, 1952.

Lisa St. Aubin **de Terán**
❏ ❏ *A Valley in Italy: The Many Seasons of a Villa in Umbria*, 1994.

Frances **Elliot**
❏ ❏ *Diary of an Idle Woman in Italy*, n. d.
(c. 1871-1872)

Jean **Giono**
❏ ❏ *An Italian Journey*, translated from the
French by John Cumming, 1998.

Maria **Grammatico** and Mary Taylor Simeti
❏ ❏ *Bitter Almonds: Recollections and Recipes
from a Sicilian Girlhood*, 1994.

Patricia **Hampl**
❏ ❏ *Virgin Time: In Search of the Contemplative
Life*, 1992.

Barbara Grizzuti **Harrison**
❏ ❏ *Italian Days*, 1989.

Katharine **Hooker**
❏ ❏ *Byways in Southern Tuscany*, 1918.

W. D. **Howells**
❏ ❏ *Italian Journeys*, 1867.

Robert J. **Hutchinson**
❏ ❏ *When in Rome: A Journal of Life in Vatican
City*, 1998.

D. H. Lawrence
❏ ❏ *Twilight in Italy*, 1916.
❏ ❏ *Sea and Sardinia*, 1921.
❏ ❏ *Etruscan Places*, 1932.

David Leavitt and Mark Mitchell
❏ ❏ *Italian Pleasures*, 1996.

Teresa Lust
❏ ❏ *Pass the Polenta: And Other Writings from the Kitchen*, 1998.

Caroline Atwater Mason
❏ ❏ *The Spell of Italy*, 1909.

Ferenc Máté
❏ ❏ *The Hills of Tuscany: A New Life in an Old Land*, 1998.

Caroline Mauduit
❏ ❏ *An Architect in Italy*, 1988.

Frances Mayes
❏ ❏ *Under the Tuscan Sun: At Home in Italy*, 1996.
❏ ❏ *Bella Tuscany: The Sweet Life in Italy*, 1999.

Joe McGinniss
❏ ❏ *The Miracle of Castel di Sangro*, 1999.

Joyce **Meyer**

❏ ❏ *Ricordi: Remembrances of Italy,* 1982.

Gary Paul **Nabhan**

❏ ❏ *Songbirds, Truffles, and Wolves: An American Naturalist in Italy,* 1993.

Eric **Newby**

❏ ❏ *A Small Place in Italy,* 1994.

Tim **Parks**

❏ ❏ *Italian Neighbors: Or, A Lapsed Anglo-Saxon in Verona,* 1992.

❏ ❏ *An Italian Education: The Further Adventures of an Expatriate in Verona,* 1995.

Daphne **Phelps**

❏ ❏ *A House in Sicily,* 1999.

Elizabeth **Romer**

❏ ❏ *The Tuscan Year: Life and Food in an Italian Valley,* 1994.

Mary Taylor **Simeti**

❏ ❏ *On Persephone's Island: A Sicilian Journal,* 1986.

Kate **Simon**

❏ ❏ *Italy: The Places in Between,* 1970.

Matthew **Spender**

❏ ❏ *Within Tuscany: Reflections on a Time and Place*, 1992.

Edith **Wharton**

❏ ❏ *Italian Villas and Their Gardens*, 1904.

❏ ❏ *Italian Backgrounds*, 1905.

Wallis **Wilde-Menozzi**

❏ ❏ *Mother Tongue: An American Life in Italy*, 1997.

GENERAL NONFICTION

Luigi **Barzini**

❏ ❏ *The Italians: A Full-Length Portrait Featuring Their Manners and Morals*, 1964.

Ann **Cornelisen**

❏ ❏ *Women of the Shadows: The Wives and Mothers of Southern Italy*, 1976.

Paul **Hofmann**

❏ ❏ *That Fine Italian Hand*, 1990.

Mary **McCarthy**

❏ ❏ *The Stones of Florence*, 1959.

❏ ❏ *Venice Observed*, 1956.

Brian **Murphy**

❏ ❏ *The New Men: Inside the Vatican's Elite School for American Priests*, 1997.

Travis **Neighbor** and Monica Larner

❏ ❏ *Living, Studying, and Working in Italy: Everything You Need to Know to Fulfill Your Dreams of Living Abroad*, 1998.

John **Ruskin**

❏ ❏ *The Stones of Venice*, 1853.

Gay **Talese**

❏ ❏ *Unto the Sons*, 1992.

GENERAL FICTION
(Also see CRIME AND MYSTERY FICTION)

Maeve **Binchy**

❏ ❏ *Evening Class*, 1996.

Joseph **Caldwell**

❏ ❏ *The Uncle from Rome*, 1992.

Pat **Conroy**

❏ ❏ *Beach Music*, 1995.

James **Cowan**

❏ ❏ *A Mapmaker's Dream: The Meditations of Fra Mauro, Cartographer to the Court of Venice*, 1996.

Martha T. **Cummings**
❏ ❏ *Straddling the Borders: The Year I Grew Up in Italy*, 1999.

Lisa St. Aubin **de Térán**
❏ ❏ *The Palace*, 1999.

Penelope **Fitzgerald**
❏ ❏ *Innocence*, 1986.

Margaret **Forster**
❏ ❏ *Lady's Maid*, 1990.

Shirley **Hazzard**
❏ ❏ *The Bay of Noon*, 1970.

Robert **Hellenga**
❏ ❏ *The Sixteen Pleasures,* 1994.

Ernest **Hemmingway**
❏ ❏ *Across the River and Into the Trees*, 1950.

Henry **James**
❏ ❏ *The Aspern Papers*, 1888.
❏ ❏ *Italian Hours*, 1909.

Valerie **Martin**
❏ ❏ *Italian Fever*, 1999.

John **Mortimer**
❏ ❏ *Summer's Lease*, 1988.

Anne **Rice**

❏ ❏ *Cry to Heaven*, 1995.

Nino **Ricco**

❏ ❏ *The Book of Saints*, 1990. (This is the first of a trilogy.)

Frank **Schaeffer**

❏ ❏ *Portofino*, 1992.

Anne Rivers **Siddons**

❏ ❏ *Hill Towns*, 1993.

Irving **Stone**

❏ ❏ *The Agony and the Ecstasy*, 1961.

Elizabeth **Von Arnim**

❏ ❏ *Enchanted April*, 1922.

Edith **Wharton**

❏ ❏ *Roman Fever and Other Stories*, with an introduction by Cynthia Griffin Wolf, 1993. Includes "Roman Fever," 1934.

CRIME AND MYSTERY FICTION

Michael **Dibdin**

❏ ❏ *A Rich, Full Death*, 1986.

❏ ❏ *Ratking*, 1989.

❏ ❏ *Dead Lagoon*, 1994.

Michael **Dibdin** (continued)

❏ ❏ *Cosi Fan Tutti*, 1996.

❏ ❏ *A Long Finish*, 1998. (Some of these are part of a series for which additional titles exist.)

Allan **Folsom**

❏ ❏ *Day of Confession*, 1998.

Robert **Girardi**

❏ ❏ *Vaporetto 13*, 1997.

John Spencer **Hill**

❏ ❏ *The Last Castrato*, 1995.

Donna **Leon**

❏ ❏ *Death at La Fenice*, 1992.

❏ ❏ *Death in a Strange Country*, 1993. (This series includes additional titles.)

William D. **Montalbano**

❏ ❏ *Basilica*, 1998.

Edward **Sklepowich**

❏ ❏ *Death in a Serene City*, 1990.

❏ ❏ *Black Bridge: A Mystery of Venice*, 1995. (This series includes additional titles.)

ITALIAN LITERATURE

Anna **Banti**
❏ ❏ *Artemisia*, translated from the Italian by Shirley D'Ardia Caracciolo, 1988.

Camillo **Boito**
❏ ❏ *Senso*, translated from the Italian by Christine Donougher, 1993.

Italo **Calvino**
❏ ❏ *Invisible Cities*, translated from the Italian by William Weaver, 1974.
❏ ❏ *Six Memos for the Millennium*, 1988 (first published in the United States).
❏ ❏ *Road to San Giovanni*, translated from the Italian by Tim Parks, 1994.

Paola **Capriolo**
❏ ❏ *Floria Tosca*, translated from the Italian by Liz Heron, 1997.

Grazia **Deledda**
❏ ❏ *Cosima*, translated from the Italian by Martha King, 1988.

Umberto **Eco**
❏ ❏ *How to Travel with a Salmon and Other Essays*, translated from the Italian by William Weaver, 1994.

Natalia **Ginzburg**

❑ ❑ *The Little Virtues*, translated from the Italian by Dick Davis, 1985.

❑ ❑ *The City and the House*, translated from the Italian by Dick Davis, 1986.

❑ ❑ *The Things We Used to Say*, translated from the Italian by Judith Woolf, 1997.

Giuseppe di **Lampedusa**

❑ ❑ *The Leopard*, translated from the Italian by Archibald Colquhoun, 1960.

Carlo **Levi**

❑ ❑ *Christ Stopped at Eboli*, translated from the Italian by Frances Frenaye, 1947.

Primo **Levi**

❑ ❑ *The Periodic Table*, translated from the Italian by Raymond Rosenthal, 1984.

❑ ❑ *The Monkey's Wrench*, translated from the Italian by William Weaver, 1986.

❑ ❑ *Other People's Trades*, translated from the Italian by Raymond Rosenthal, 1989.

Rosetta **Loy**

❑ ❑ *The Dust Roads of Monferrato*, translated from the Italian by William Weaver, 1990.

Niccolò **Machiavelli**

❑ ❑ *The Prince*, translated from the Italian by Luigi Ricci, 1903.

Anna Maria **Ortese**

❑ ❑ *The Iguana*, translated from the Italian by Henry Martin, 1987.

Cesare **Pavese**

❑ ❑ *The Moon and the Bonfire*, translated from the Italian by Louise Sinclair, 1952.

Susanna **Tamaro**

❑ ❑ *Follow Your Heart*, translated from the Italian by John Cullen, 1995.

Sebastiano **Vassalli**

❑ ❑ *The Swan*, translated from the Italian by Emma Rose, 1997.

Acknowledgements

Special thanks to my editor, Susan Luton of Austin. And *mille grazie* to the dozens of other friends and family members who have been patient and understanding of the writing process!

Our readers are important to us. We'd love to hear your ideas and suggestions: missed movies and books, more ways to feed an Italy fever!

Books are available at special quantity discounts for bulk purchases for sales promotions, premiums, and fund-raising. Additional Italy Fever products are also available. Please visit our Web site.

www.italyfever.com

Portico Press, Inc.
P. O. Box 1337
Fredericksburg, TX 78624

Fax (830) 990-9588
E-mail: PorticoPress@italyfever.com

About the Author

Darlene Marwitz holds two master's degrees from the School of Architecture at The University of Texas in Austin. She worked for six years on the historic preservation and restoration of the Texas Capitol before returning to private business. She lives in Austin and Fredericksburg with her husband David. This is her first book.